A Marriage at Sea

Praise for *A Marriage at Sea*

A NEW YORK TIMES TOP 10 BOOK OF 2025

ONE OF PRESIDENT BARACK OBAMA'S FAVORITE BOOKS OF 2025

WINNER OF THE OUTDOOR BOOK AWARD

NAMED A BEST BOOK OF THE YEAR BY: NPR, *TIME, PEOPLE MAGAZINE, THE NEW YORKER, VOGUE, FRESH AIR, USA TODAY, SLATE, TOWN & COUNTRY, VOGUE, VOX, REAL SIMPLE*, AND MANY MORE

"*A Marriage at Sea* was such an emotionally vivid portrait of a couple in isolation that I was shocked it wasn't fiction. How could a writer get so deeply into the minds of two real people in such extraordinary circumstances? Brilliantly depicted." —*ELLE*

"This book took my breath away—almost literally at times . . . one of the most delightfully nerve-wracking books I've read in a long time. There is an innate engine to a survival tale, and *A Marriage at Sea* is no different. But it also goes beyond that, examining what it takes for an individual and a marriage to survive such an extreme test . . . a feat of reporting and storytelling." —*Vogue*

"Elegant and propulsive . . . I found myself, alternately, holding my breath as I read at top speed, wandering rooms in search of someone to read aloud to, and placing the book facedown, arrested by quiet statements that left me reeling with their depth."

—*The New York Times Book Review*

"Gripping . . . To say Elmhirst's book is nail-bitingly tense at times is an understatement. . . . But aside from all the adrenaline boosting and gory reports of oozing butt sores, rancid meat and lack of potable water, part of what makes *A Marriage at Sea* so compulsively readable is Elmhirst's meditation on the Bailey's relationship as their marriage is put to the ultimate test. A propulsive, perceptive portrait of two lovers literally adrift at sea—and the ties that keep bringing them back together, against all odds."

—*San Francisco Chronicle*

"A transfixing, beautiful work, its deeper currents steering us forward, whether we realize it or not." —*The Wall Street Journal*

"Enthralling . . . Elmhirst sets her reader down inside a world that is both tiny and vast, at once ruthlessly monotonous and violently unpredictable." —*The New Yorker*

"The book I've recommended to more people than any other in 2025 is this riveting tale of adventure—and the true story isn't even the best part of it. . . . What makes *A Marriage at Sea* (note the double meaning in that title) special is Elmhirst's writing. As harrowing and gripping as the Baileys' story is, the real star of this book is its dazzling writer. Elmhirst succeeds at everything she attempts. . . . Just about every moment in *A Marriage at Sea* is full of drama and tension." —*The Minnesota Star Tribune*

"Amazing true story of a couple surviving crisis in the open seas."

—President Barack Obama

"This is the gripping and unforgettable tale of how they endured illness, dehydration, near-starvation, and every emotion on the spectrum and managed to stay married for decades after. It's an unbelievable story masterfully told." —*Book Riot*

"A gripping tale of survival and a testament to the power of love." —*People*

"Elegant and electric . . . In Elmhirst's hands, the story of the Baileys' ordeal becomes a portrait of a marriage: how two people can drive each other to the edges of despair, and how they can keep each other alive in a time of almost unimaginable horror." —*Vox*

"The suspense during *Marriage at Sea* is painful yet riveting. It's a horror movie. The end can't come fast enough, yet there is also no looking away. Although at its heart this book is about survival and love, it's also a transcendent rumination on what marriages are, and should be." —*Pittsburgh Post-Gazette*

"Gird your loins and line up your couple's therapist." —*The New York Times Book Review* podcast

"So deeply intimate . . . a gripping exploration of adversity. . . . Elmhirst has written a truly gripping "memoir" about survival, but what's most compelling is her exploration of love, marriage, and mindset." —*Goop*

"Few nonfiction books get a reader's adrenaline pumping quite like Sophie Elmhirst's *A Marriage at Sea.*" —*The Washington Post*

"An enthralling, engrossing story of survival and the resilience of the human spirit . . . a nonfiction work that reaches the highest literary eminence." —*New York Times* bestselling author Bill Bryson

"Stark, elemental, and sure to be a classic, Sophie Elmhirst's beautifully written tale suggests that perhaps the only thing more difficult than braving the high seas is navigating the vicissitudes of marriage . . . while keeping one's sanity intact."

—*New York Times* bestselling author Hampton Sides

"Sophie Elmhirst distills the rollicking tale of the near-death adventure of an English couple on the high seas into something that is somehow more than the sum of its parts: a beautiful meditation on endurance, codependence, and the power of love. A dazzling book."

—*New York Times* bestselling author Patrick Radden Keefe

"A mysterious, beautiful book about fate and marriage and the kind of loneliness that is honored and nourished rather than avoided. Sophie Elmhirst manages to illustrate the ways in which committing to a loving relationship—while shipwrecked or not—can become a matter of survival."

—*New York Times* bestselling author Rachel Aviv

A Marriage at Sea

A TRUE STORY *of* LOVE, OBSESSION, *and* SHIPWRECK

Sophie Elmhirst

RIVERHEAD BOOKS
NEW YORK

RIVERHEAD BOOKS
An imprint of Penguin Random House LLC
1745 Broadway, New York, NY 10019
penguinrandomhouse.com

Book design and illustrations by Meighan Cavanaugh

The Library of Congress has Cataloged the Hardcover Edition as Follows:

Names: Elmhirst, Sophie, author.
Title: A marriage at sea: A true story of love, obsession, and shipwreck / Sophie Elmhirst.
Description: New York: Riverhead Books, 2025.
Identifiers: LCCN 2024041610 (print) | LCCN 2024041611 (ebook) |
ISBN 9780593854280 (hardcover) | ISBN 9780593854303 (ebook)
Subjects: LCSH: Bailey, Maurice. | Bailey, Maralyn. | Shipwrecks—Pacific Ocean. |
Shipwreck survival—Pacific Ocean. | Shipwreck victims—Pacific Ocean—Biography. |
Married people—Biography.
Classification: LCC G530.B15 E56 2025 (print) | LCC G530.B15 (ebook) |
DDC 910.9164—dc23/eng/20250210
LC record available at https://lccn.loc.gov/2024041610
LC ebook record available at https://lccn.loc.gov/2024041611

First published in hardcover in Great Britain as *Maurice and Maralyn: A Whale, a Shipwreck, a Love Story* by Chatto & Windus, an imprint of Penguin Random House Ltd., London, in 2024.
First United States edition published by Riverhead, 2025.

First Riverhead hardcover edition: July 2025
First Riverhead trade paperback edition: June 2026
Riverhead trade paperback ISBN: 9780593854297

Printed in the United States of America
1st Printing

The authorized representative in the EU for product safety and compliance is Penguin Random House Ireland, Morrison Chambers, 32 Nassau Street, Dublin D02 YH68, Ireland, https://eu-contact.penguin.ie.

To my mother,

and in memory of my father

Part One

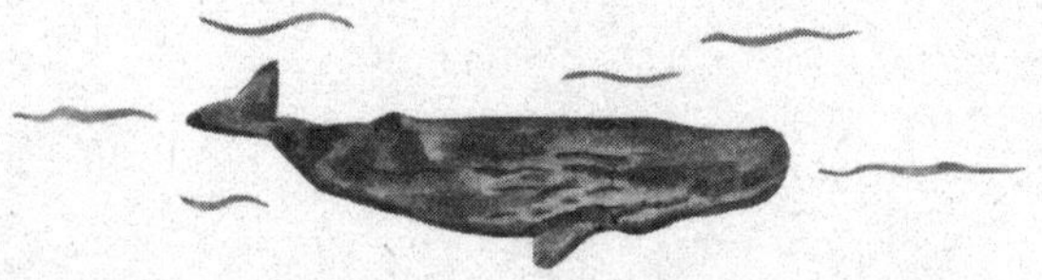

ONE

4 March 1973

Maralyn looked out at emptiness. There was little to see except the water, shifting from black to blue as the sun rose. A clear sky, the ocean, and themselves: a small boat, sailing west.

At seven o'clock, Maralyn left her watch on deck and went down to the cabin. Maurice was still asleep in his bunk, stirring a little. The morning would follow the certain rhythms of every other morning: coffee and breakfast, then all the checks and jobs a boat requires. A formula so practised after months at sea that it had become as automatic as time.

Except this morning, in the precise moment that Maralyn put her hand on Maurice to wake him, they felt a crack, a jolt, the sound of a gun going off, as if the violence had come from her touch. The noise split the air. Books leapt off the shelves. Cutlery flew.

They thought of their boat as their child. To hear her wood tear and splinter was like hearing the pained scream of an infant.

Up on deck, they discovered the cause. A whale was next to them in the ocean, massive and alive. Water was streaming down the dark cliffs of its body as it twisted and writhed. It looked as if it were trying to climb out of the waves, hauling its dark bulk up, then smashing back down, a meteor landing in the ocean, showering spray. Its tail, ten feet across the flukes, was beating at the surface in a kind of fury. Blood poured from its body into the water.

Maralyn couldn't understand where it had come from. She'd just been up here, waiting for the dawn, and seen nothing but a fishing boat when she'd taken over from Maurice at three. You don't miss a whale.

But perhaps you do. It must have risen from the depths just after she'd gone down the ladder and broken the surface right where they were. She couldn't bear the thought that they'd somehow hurt the creature. It seemed uncanny that in the entirety of the Pacific this would be the spot it chose.

What did it matter? There it was. A sperm whale, Maurice could tell, from the blunt, square block of its head. He knew his whales. It was forty feet long, he guessed; a good ten feet longer than their boat.

This close, it was difficult to take in. Whales were best admired from a distance, like certain kinds of paintings. He could identify its parts—the blowhole, the lower jaw, the pectoral fin—but they didn't seem to add up to a coherent whole. The creature was out of proportion, unnatural in its size. One rogue swipe of its tail and they would be cleaved in two. It was monstrous, he thought. Only compared with them.

The whale was still thrashing, as if it were trying to shake something off, or escape its own body. It was dying, Maurice realised. These were its death throes.

And then it was gone, sucked into the unknown darkness of the ocean. It would likely die down there, blood leaking into the water, alerting other creatures to its presence. Great whites and blue sharks would gather, rip it apart, and feast on its blubber.

They stared at where it had been, the surface marked by dissolving trails of blood. Such stillness, after a performance like that.

~

Wait. The crack. Never mind the *whale*.

Down in the cabin, water was already coming up through the floorboards. How long had they wasted up on deck, staring at the whale! Maralyn worked the pump while Maurice splashed around searching for the damage. There it was: a hole below the waterline near the galley, about eighteen inches long, twelve inches wide, the size of a briefcase.

Maurice was shouting. Get the spare jib sheet. Clip it to the corner of the head sail. Lower it over the bow and drag it to cover the hole, then make it fast at both ends to secure it. The pressure from the ocean should force the sheet into the hole, plugging it. He adjusted the sails to keep the boat moving at about two to three knots, and they hurried back down below deck.

Maralyn kept pumping, hoping the water level would now go down. But the sheet wasn't working; the water kept rising. They needed a way of plugging the leak from the inside. Maralyn found clothes, cushions, and blankets and stuffed them into the hole. That didn't work either. Perhaps there was another hole they hadn't found. Some unseen damage where the water was pouring in. It was too late to find it now. The water was up to their knees, and the cupboards were starting to spring open, unleashing their contents. Eggs and tins bobbed around them. They looked at each other.

Maurice fetched the life raft and the dinghy, then collected as many freshwater containers as he could find. Maralyn waded round the galley, filling two sail bags with their things. Two plastic bowls, a bucket, their emergency bag, passports, a camera, a torch, their oilskins, her diary, two books, two dictionaries, and Maurice's navigational tools: his *Nautical Almanac* and *Sight Reduction Tables*, his chart, sextant, compass, and logbook.

They worked fast and in silence, strangely calm as the water rose. It wasn't easy, gathering possessions from a vessel filling with ocean. Ten minutes, it took, to gather what they could. Then they climbed off the boat into the dinghy.

Around them the Pacific was moving gently. Maralyn watched cushions she'd spent hours embroidering float away on the waves. Their boat settled low in the ocean, then lower.

Maralyn found her camera and took a picture of Maurice, who was sitting in front of her, shirtless. He turned back to look at her, every muscle of his back delineated under the harsh glare of the sun, wearing an expression not of fear, not yet, but of a kind of taut blankness, as if he had not quite grasped what was taking place, the sight of their boat tipping to one side as she sank in the middle of the ocean.

She went down so gracefully. The solid bulk of her hull, the deck, cockpit, sails, and ropes all quietly swallowed by the water. Maralyn took a picture as the last triangle of sail and the tip of the mast disappeared beneath the surface. Frozen in the photograph, the mast looked as if it might be coming the other way, emerging from the water like a thin arm hoping for rescue.

TWO

Maurice Bailey, in 1962, was working as a compositor at Bemrose printers in Derby, a fine old press that in its prime had printed the large railway timetables pinned up on station notice boards across England. Maurice arranged blocks of text in mirror image on the slate, a technical job that required long training, an exacting eye, and the ability to read upside down.

In the evenings, he returned home to a cramped flat on Rose Hill Street, a thin road of squat, redbrick houses near the centre of the city. Halfway down the road was a reminder of how a different class of Derby had once lived: A grand manor with pea-green gates and square chimneys overlooked the Derby Arboretum, a gift to the city from Joseph Strutt, a nineteenth-century mill owner, grateful to the local workers for making his fortune.

Like much of England, Derby was in the middle of a building spree. Council estates and suburbs were spreading at its edges. A looping sequence of ring roads and roundabouts were being constructed to encircle its old Tudor heart.

Maurice didn't much like the place. He called Derby a backwater, a city where nothing happened.

The people were unworldly, he felt, judgemental of anything that seemed to threaten their own existence. In a letter to a friend, he noticed how families newly arrived in his neighbourhood from the Caribbean were greeted with "brutish racism." He escaped whenever he could, driving up to the hills of the Peak District, where he went rock climbing or flying in small planes. He played tennis, too, and lifted weights at a local gym to improve his tennis. And he sailed.

Maurice's hobbies were not just distraction. They gave him a sense of freedom, of a life beyond the limits of his own. Other than work, he had little else. For years he had been alone in the stubborn sort of way that lodges in people when they can't imagine sharing their life with someone else. "A pattern of detached bachelorhood," as he put it. He never saw his family, who lived only a few miles away in their end-of-terrace house in Spondon, a quiet village east of Derby.

Maurice's father was Charles, but everyone called him Jack. When he wasn't working at the Rolls-Royce factory down the road, he had his hobbies, growing vegetables out back and ringing bells in local churches on the weekends. Maurice's mother, Annie, had once been in service, working at a large house in Spondon. She stopped to bring up the four children she had over two decades: Reg, the eldest, then Maurice, Joan, and, last of all, Bob. Their births bracketed the Second World War: Maurice was born in 1933, Bob in 1947, into a different world.

Four children of the same parents do not receive the same parenting. Maurice was unlucky. He had a stutter and a hunched back, then caught tuberculosis before there was effective treatment. Annie's ginger hair turned white overnight, she always said. To recover, Maurice had to stay in bed for months, alone in his room. It can stay with you, time like that; conditioning loneliness, baking it in.

Maurice became a problem to be fixed. He'd missed so much school being ill that he had to spend weeks catching up. Later, he told friends that Annie had made him copy out the dictionary, standing over him with a ruler in her hand to swat him if he made a mistake. It wasn't so unusual then for parents not to kiss or cuddle their children, but that didn't make the absence of affection any easier to bear.

The silent room, the stutter, the ruler—they did their work. Maurice, as a teenager, couldn't bear himself. He was mortified by how he looked and how he was. He became awkward around people, hobbled by self-consciousness. Aged fourteen, in his Spondon House Secondary School photograph, he stood a head taller than almost everyone else. With his hooded eyes and solemn expression he looked a weary forty compared with the thin-legged, bright-faced girls and boys around him.

All he wanted was to escape. His first attempt was intellectual. Annie had been brought up in a strictly Christian household, had it stuffed down her throat, she said. While she no longer went to church, she made her children go, just in case, like an insurance policy. Faith wasn't about belief as much as behaviour. Sunday school and reading the Bible—it was what you did and it made you good.

Maurice, rebelling, discovered science. He read about the origins of the universe and natural selection and decided that the theory of evolution made much more sense than Christian theology. He voiced his reservations; his parents objected. It was as if he were trying to dismantle morality.

So he left. Two years of military service in Egypt and he came out a sergeant. Then home again, for evening classes. He only ever came into the living room to eat. Otherwise, he kept himself apart from his family as much as he could. He had a Morris Minor, a small car that was good for getting away, and took his younger brother, Bob, up to the Peak District to go walking. They climbed Kinder Scout. Maurice would tease Bob, which Bob hated, but it was only the natural order of things, the way families pass down pain like an inheritance.

Once Maurice had his job and his flat in Derby, he was gone for good. To Bob, it seemed as if he wanted to start again, to pretend his childhood had never happened. They hardly saw him after that. He never spoke of them. Years later, he turned up at his father's cremation. He didn't go to his mother's funeral at all.

~

Once a month, on a Sunday, there was a local car rally in Derby. Mike, an acquaintance of Maurice's from the gym, asked Maurice if he'd like to go along in his place. Mike usually went with a colleague from the Derby tax office but he couldn't make it this week, and she wanted a companion.

Maurice panicked. He was nervous around new people, and he knew nothing about cars. Generally, he liked to do things that he'd done before. This was the kind of situation he'd ruin, just by being himself.

Mike reassured him. You'll be fine, he said, not knowing Maurice very well.

On Sunday morning, Maurice waited at the agreed spot, the Market Place in the centre of Derby, overlooked by the old clock tower, bells ringing out the hour. Cars kept passing and slowing. He watched with relief as they drove on. Perhaps she wouldn't turn up. Then a car stopped in front of him, a large Vauxhall Cresta driven by a young woman with long dark hair. She wore jeans and a blue sweater and smiled up at him. Maralyn.

What was it? The casual way she leant across the seat to open the passenger door. The ease with which she smiled. Her vigorous driving towards the start of the rally. She seemed to know instinctively how to *do* things, a way of being that was at odds with Maurice's conception of what people, or at least himself, were generally like. She could talk, just talk, even while driving. And the Cresta was something in itself. A four-door carpeted saloon, bench seats and heater fitted as standard, modelled on the American Buick with tail fins and white-walled tyres. Pure chutzpah. It made the Morris Minor look parochial.

Maurice crumbled. If you believe you're a disaster before

you've even begun, it tends to go that way. Everything he said was wrong. He was supposed to be navigating as she drove, but he kept confusing left and right. When he tried to correct his mistakes, he made things worse. At the end of the day he offered to buy petrol for the car, but when he put his hand in his pocket, he had only ten shillings and fourpence. Maralyn had to pay.

How did he not have the money? It seemed absurd, yet somehow inevitable. Like all practised self-saboteurs, everything he did seemed only to confirm the abject opinion he already had of himself. "That was the end of it," he wrote later. "My first contact with this wonderful girl was to be my last."

A formal apology was called for. He wrote Maralyn a letter and sent her the largest bunch of flowers he could afford. A few days later, to his surprise, she replied, thanking him. Mike, on subtle questioning, revealed that Maralyn was just a colleague, nothing more. Maurice wrote to her again, asking her out. Maralyn replied, not by return post, but by calling Maurice at work. The boldness of it! Just ringing him up like that at the press, as if that were a normal or acceptable thing to do. Maurice had to pretend it was a business call.

~

Their first evening together, Maurice took her to a Chinese restaurant. They drank wine, then went to the theatre. Maralyn had never done any of these things before. She was only twenty-one and still living with her parents, Fred and Ada, in their home in Normanton, south of Derby's centre. Fred and Ada were Maralyn's uncle and aunt who'd adopted Maralyn after her mother, Mary, Ada's sister, got divorced. Maralyn became their only child. They were protective over her, kept her world small. Maurice liked the feeling of introducing her to things.

Later, they drove back to her house and she asked him in. They whispered to each other for hours while her parents slept. She told him the short story of her life: Parkfields Cedars Grammar School for girls, then teacher training, a brief stint at a private school in Shrewsbury, her job in the Derby tax office. Beyond work, her life mostly revolved around her parents: baking with Ada, listening to Fred play his trumpet in a local band. Her biological mother, Mary, remarried and had two more children, Patricia and Brian. As half sisters, Pat and Maralyn became close. Pat often came round to Maralyn's on weekends: playing in the garden as children, listening to music and Radio Luxembourg as they grew up. Later, Pat would try to persuade Maralyn to go to dances at the local barracks, but Maralyn always said no. She didn't seem interested in the things that busied her peers. It wasn't out of timidity, more that she preferred to be outside, going for walks. She never put on makeup or minded what she wore. Pat used to give her castoffs, the only fashionable things Maralyn ever owned. Early in the morning, the sky still dark and the streets empty and silent, Maurice and Maralyn crept out of the house to the Cresta and slept together on its wide bench seat. A seat, Maurice noted later, that made it "an excellent courting vehicle." As the sky grew light, they drove out of the city. In the open country they stopped by the side of the road and walked through a field of long grass, dew soaking their feet.

Maralyn showed Maurice where to find newly sprouting mushrooms and explained their life cycle, how their threadlike mycelium forms a network through the soil connecting everything that grows. Maurice marvelled that she knew such things.

THREE

Love, when it works, can feel like such a terrifying fluke. Two people have to choose and be chosen, and, most unlikely of all, these choices must happen at roughly the same time. Why Maurice chose Maralyn was obvious. "I needed someone like Maralyn in my life to make up for the confidence I lacked," he wrote. She coloured in his gaps.

Why Maralyn chose Maurice seemed more perplexing, at least at first. Pat always thought that Maralyn could have had anyone she wanted. She was so confident and pretty, so at ease in herself. Maurice was sure she must have other suitors. Her life was just starting to open out. Maurice, nearly thirty, had narrowed his to a dark flat and a low opinion of himself. Loneliness had closed around him like a case.

But Maralyn was stuck too. Fred and Ada liked the old ways, things done properly. Fred worked on the railways; Ada, who'd worked in service, had standards. When Pat visited, she and Maralyn were put to work by Ada: shelling peas, polishing the brass knocker on the front door, scrubbing the front step with a donkey stone. As the seasons changed, they swapped winter curtains for summer ones. Maralyn would not leave home until she was married.

Then what? Cooking, cleaning, children: the domestic formula. But Maralyn wasn't Ada; the cyclical work of a home wasn't enough. She liked to push at the limits of things, according to Pat. Before she met Maurice, she used to smoke Stuyvesants, the long ones with a tip. She liked large, flashy cars, and was the kind of person who drove her Cresta to rallies on the weekends; who had no qualms about ringing up a man she liked at his office. Beyond the confines of her parents' house and the Derby tax office, she sensed the possibility of a different kind of life. Here was a man, nine years older, who already appeared to be living it, sailing boats and climbing mountains. He flew *planes*.

~

As soon as he could, Maurice took Maralyn out to the hills. He wanted her to try climbing and flying, to like what he liked, but it was also a kind of test. Would she manage up a mountain; would she love it as much as he did? It was satisfying, showing her things he was good at. Maralyn didn't take to flying, but she did turn out to be a sturdy walker, unafraid of bad weather. Maurice took her to the Lake District, where they camped in a farmer's field. It was Easter but still so cold that it snowed. He worried she might be put off, but she never complained or suggested they pack up and go home. After a day's hiking, they returned to their tent, frozen. Maralyn declared that they would eat the first thing she could find in their box of provisions and warmed up a pan of custard over their Primus stove. She didn't even ask him what he wanted: She already seemed to know.

She showed the same flair on mountain ascents. Maurice purposefully took her on a difficult route up Yr Wyddfa on a hot day, and Maralyn stripped off her top to walk in her bra, not minding who saw. When they climbed Ben Nevis, she insisted they reach the summit even once they were enveloped by mist and wind. They ran back down holding hands to escape the storm and spent the whole night awake, clinging to the tent's poles to stop it from flying away.

During that first year together, Maralyn had her own test for Maurice: a week's holiday with her parents in Cumbria. Maralyn drove them up from Derby in the Cresta, and on the way home suggested that Maurice have a turn at the wheel. Maurice found himself going a hundred miles an hour down the A1. Fred and Ada sat in the back, locked in what Maurice took to be an unhappy silence. If the trip was meant to seek their blessing, he didn't think he'd been successful. But Maralyn didn't mind: better, surely, to spend her future alongside someone who drove a hundred miles an hour than to stay stuck in the backseat with her parents.

Of all the new pursuits, Maurice wanted Maralyn's first sailing trip to be a triumph. That summer, he rented a twenty-six-foot boat on the Norfolk Broads, a network of inland rivers and lakes a few hours' drive to the east of Derby. Maralyn didn't know how to swim, but that didn't seem to put them off. Maurice began to teach her how to sail, and after a few days he judged she was ready to operate the tiller on her own. Everything went well until they ploughed at speed into a riverbank. Maurice, chastising himself, had forgotten her "novice status," as he put it. They spent the afternoon digging out the boat with knives and forks, teased by passersby.

~

Maurice knew he wanted to marry her. Of course he did. For so long he'd been convinced his bachelorhood was a permanent state. Maralyn had opened a door. But there was a problem: He would have to ask. Maurice thought she'd say no, presuming he was the latest in a line of men with the same idea and surely not the best of them. "Not often in my life has there been a time when I found sufficient resolve to overcome, hesitatingly and with quaking diffidence, my stifling social inhibitions," he wrote. Maurice always had so much to wade through before he could *do* anything. But he asked, and she said yes. Not just any kind of yes, but a clear, certain yes, as if she'd never had a doubt.

Her acceptance opened up a new seam of worry.

What did marriage actually entail? Change, certainly. Expectations that might differ; adjustments to another person and their own notions about how life might be lived. Maurice had lived a decade according to his own precise rhythm. It was difficult for him to imagine bending to someone else.

There were particular things, too, that he simply would not

tolerate. He did not want a religious ceremony; nor did he want to give up his hobbies. Most of all, he didn't want children, determined that his genetic line should end with him, as though he didn't want to perpetuate a mistake.

In 1962, this felt like a rare and controversial position. Britain was still a country shadowed by war. Rationing had ended only eight years before. The assumed aspirations for a young couple were security and prosperity, a brace of cheerful children in a tidy home.

"It's not that I don't *like* children," Maurice would say when people asked. But the truth was that he didn't actually like them very much. Small ones struck him as noisy and self-centred, teenagers as presumptuous and overconfident. He found himself awkward around all of them. It had been hard enough being a child himself; he'd clawed his way out of the state as quickly as he could. Why would he choose to inflict it on someone else? Maurice was not a father, he argued, for the same reason he was not a nuclear physicist or an astronaut: "I try not to do things I cannot do well." To his delight, Maralyn agreed to everything. She had no interest in a religious wedding. As for his hobbies, apart from flying she wanted to do them all too. Being up in the hills and out on the water had woken something in her. She'd tasted adventure, seen what the world could offer.

Most miraculously of all, she didn't want children either. They knew that people assumed they had a physical problem, too shameful to be admitted, or considered them selfish. But, bolstered by Maralyn, Maurice no longer minded what other people thought. To deal with tactless questions from new acquaintances, or from people mystified by the idea that childlessness might be a choice, Maralyn came up with a joke: "Maurice is problem enough without having children."

~

On 21 December 1963, they were married. The ceremony took place at the Derby Register Office off the Market Place, where Maralyn had first pulled up in the Cresta. It was a small affair, with few guests, just Fred, Ada, and Mary. No one from Maurice's family was invited. Maralyn went as she was: There was no special dress.

Afterwards, they had sandwiches at their newly bought home, a bungalow in the Derby suburb of Allestree. Pat went along, but didn't stay long. Maurice made it clear: If the guests wanted a drink, they'd have to go out. He was often like that with Maralyn: fending people off. Pat always felt he wanted her to himself.

The new bungalow had been bought off-plan a few months before with a loan from the Derbyshire Building Society. It stood in a row of identical bungalows, small and redbrick, with two large windows either side of the front door, like a mouthless face. It was a model home, exactly the kind of place a newly married couple should move into. Allestree had all the right things for decent, family-minded people: a church, a school, and a cricket club. There were cul-de-sacs named after trees (ash, oak, thorn, larch); front gardens bordered by low walls; and garages for nearly all.

For weeks before the wedding, Maralyn had been collecting extra bits and pieces, crockery and cutlery, in a large bin in her bedroom, as Ada had done before her own marriage. Now they could lay it all out, assign everything to its rightful place. Their life was smoothed by things they'd never owned before: central heating, a telephone, a washing machine. They had new furniture and carpets, too, chosen on regular trips to Nottingham. They tended their garden, and started a fund to buy their own boat, putting aside some of Maurice's salary every month. After the mortgage, there was little to spare out of either of their wages, but it was something.

~

Perhaps it was just a feeling, a low hum. Or perhaps it was because Allestree was a place where a particular kind of quiet stiffened the air and lives unfolded behind securely locked front doors, where safety was not only desired but inescapable. Or perhaps it was because the liberating shift of the late sixties was still a way off. Whatever it was, as the years passed, they grew restless.

Maurice still found Derby stultifying. Their home, with all its new machines, represented the "formula of suburban domestic stress," he wrote. His job, secure as it was, felt like the "mechanical slavery of everyday employment." Their habits were shaped by postwar austerity. They were thrifty, grew their own vegetables, threw nothing away that could be repurposed. Yes, they had a washing machine, but it wasn't enough. "We knew," Maurice wrote later, "with the same certainty that Newton had for his theory about gravity, that our affluent, though mundane, life would not satisfy us forever."

On a wet November evening in 1966, Maralyn stared out the

window as raindrops chased each other down the glass. It was damp and cold and dark, everyone tucked up in their houses for the long night, curtains drawn.

"Suppose," she said to Maurice, "that we sold our house, bought a yacht, and lived on board."

It sounded absurd. Why would they sell the house they'd only just managed to buy? Admittedly, it was the only way they'd ever be able to own a boat. Prices of yachts were rising faster than wages, and they'd saved only a tiny amount of Maurice's earnings. But still, they weren't the kinds of rash people who sold their home. At least Maurice wasn't. He felt stifled by domesticity and work, but that was just *life*. They had achieved what they were supposed to achieve. They were safe on their own patch of land. You don't mock such hard-won stability. You certainly don't sell it off.

"You're not even trying," said Maralyn.

In the grip of an idea, Maralyn could drill through rock. Plans emerged, as if already fully formed and inarguable. A boat was around £3,000 and the bungalow was worth about the same. Once they'd sold up and paid off the mortgage, they could afford to start building a boat straightaway. They'd have to do it slowly, saving everything they earned.

And then, well, *then* they'd sail round the world, to New Zealand. More people lived on the south coast of England than in the whole of New Zealand, Maralyn pointed out. The Lake District was tame and overrun by comparison. They would be like pioneers, discovering new lands on the other side of the world. And what land: rugged and empty and wild. As a friend put it later, it was as if she thought it might still be uninhabited.

It wasn't only New Zealand. Think of the journey, all the places they could stop on the way: the Canaries, the Caribbean, the Galápagos. They would be real travellers, real explorers, free—as only a boat allows—to go wherever they liked, whenever they liked. No one overseeing them, no one knowing where they were. They could leave England and never come back. Maralyn, struck by the idea of nature on a scale and in forms she'd never seen in the tidy back gardens of England, began compiling a scrapbook of New Zealand's flora and fauna.

To leave England and never come back. For Maurice, it was revelatory. To start again. To shed everything that England contained: his past, his family, himself. It is an irresistible thought, that we might be someone different somewhere else.

Maurice applied for a job in Wellington, the capital of New Zealand, and received a tentative offer. "In short," he wrote later, "her arguments finally won me over."

~

You don't just build a boat and go. The planning is everything. Maurice studied books of ocean passages and pilot charts and reread the closest thing he had to a sacred text, the sailor Eric Hiscock's guide to circumnavigating the globe, *Voyaging Under Sail*.

The classic route was southwest, across the Bay of Biscay to Spain, then to Madeira, the Canary Islands, then twenty-seven hundred miles across the Atlantic, through the Caribbean and the Panama Canal, then across the Pacific to the Galápagos, another long ocean crossing to the Marquesas Islands, the Tuamotu Islands, Fiji, and finally to New Zealand. To avoid the worst of the tropical storms, Hiscock suggested they leave England in the summer in time to catch the trade winds that would propel them across the Atlantic, enabling them to arrive in the Caribbean after mid-November and leave again in the new year. With stop-offs along the way, and allowing for delays, they could expect to be in New Zealand the following autumn.

Maralyn wrote out a timetable, estimating how long it would take for a boat to be built and fitted out in preparation for the voyage. They knew what they wanted. A wooden boat, minimum thirty feet long. To the novice eye, a classic, small sailing boat, the kind you might see cruising along an easy stretch of the south coast for an afternoon, not crossing the Pacific.

According to Hiscock, seaworthiness, comfort, and speed were the most important features, *in that order.* Vital, too, if the crew was to be small, was a boat that was easy to handle and able to steer herself. She should be sturdy enough to sail across oceans and through violent weather while weighed down by hundreds of tins of food and containers of water.

Maurice and Maralyn picked out a model, a Golden Hind, a thirty-one-foot Bermuda sloop, named after the galleon Sir Francis Drake sailed into Plymouth Harbour in 1580, stuffed with cloves and treasure stolen from Spanish colonies and ships on the west coast of South America. The first iterations of the new Golden Hind had recently been built by Hartwell's in Plymouth, a firm of coffin makers looking to expand their range. While she wasn't fast, she was solid, or "stiff in a blow" as her specifications stated. Her reliability had gained her a reputation as the Morris Minor of the yachting world, which seemed fitting.

Maurice and Maralyn commissioned Hartwell's to build their own version, for delivery in the spring of 1968. They requested certain modifications: a moderate draught, full headroom, ample beam, high freeboard, and a galvanised steel wind vane, for steering, bolted to the deck. On board, they would have no radio transmitter or extraneous electronic devices of any kind.

Everyone thought they were mad. *No radio transmitter*? But Maurice wanted to "preserve their freedom from outside interference." To feel truly alone on the ocean, he chose to sail the old way, by his wits and the stars. It was elevating, moving, even, to know that he was relying on the same constellations that had guided the great captains before him: Columbus, Cook. The centuries fell away when he was looking up as they had done, seeing what they had seen. And what purity there would be in sailing like this, just him and Maralyn needing no one but each other and the sky above. "The worldly-wise at home ridiculed us, or smiled patronisingly at us," wrote Maurice. "And of course who is to say they were not right?" But who cared if they were? All those people whose narrowness was born of a life on land, who knew nothing but the cosy oppressions of middle-class England. They were half the reason he was leaving in the first place.

~

A project as long, expensive, and complicated as building a boat in Plymouth could not be overseen from Derby, nearly three hundred miles north and a place as far from the sea as any you could find in England. Maralyn proposed they move south, to Southampton, from where they would eventually sail.

Maurice moved first, finding work at Camelot Press, a firm of book printers on Shirley Road in the west of the city. He rented a cheap, unfurnished flat nearby and slept on the hard floor, cooked on a camping stove under bare lightbulbs, and ate alone at a card table. It was a bit like Rose Hill Street: a meagre, lonely existence. But this was different. Maralyn would be joining him.

Maralyn, meanwhile, stayed in Derby and sold off the furniture. Maurice went up on weekends to visit, grateful to sleep in a bed again, until she sold that too. All those things they'd chosen in the Nottingham shops, all gone. Sailing tends to be full of people with money. Maurice and Maralyn were not those people. The boat took everything they had.

Once the house was sold, Maralyn moved south and got a job at the Southampton tax office. She tried to soften the edges of the Shirley flat, rigging up some curtains. But she stopped short of buying a bed. There seemed little point given that they'd only have to sell it again. They slept on the floor.

In 1968 their boat was ready enough to be sailed. From the shipbuilders' in Plymouth they steered her through the choppy waters off the south coast to Moody's Boatyard on the Hamble River and moved on board. The Shirley flat was luxurious by comparison: The inside of the boat was not yet fitted out, and they lived among timber and tools and the general filth of construction. They gave her a name: *Auralyn*, a combination of theirs. Maralyn's idea.

The work on the boat's interior took them four years. Four

years, 1968 to 1972, in which England segued from one decade to another and one prime minister to the next, Harold Wilson to Ted Heath. House prices were beginning their steady ascent, quadrupling from the beginning of the seventies to the end. Many of the couple's peers, who'd bought their homes in the sixties, found themselves becoming rich by default.

Maurice and Maralyn realised, with a certain pride, that they were taking a different path. "For us," Maurice wrote, "prosaic and worldly things—money, property and self-interest—from which men build their castles of vanity and power, meant nothing."

But like all utopian visions, theirs had its contradictions. They'd sold all their belongings to build a boat. They were abandoning everyone they knew to live afloat, alone, unshackled from obligation and community, from all the things that bind a person to a place or its people, from the day-to-day indignities of ordinary life and the unseen rules whose weight perhaps you feel only in the place you were raised. After all, what is more self-interested than running away?

~

Moody's Boatyard was a friendly place. Rows of yachts, large and small, lived in the marina next door, waiting for their time at sea. Ropes and masts clanked and tapped in the breeze. Sailors hopped on and off each other's boats, offering help. All around was a kind of anticipatory energy, a sense that time on land was a stopgap, a necessary boredom, until you were sailing again.

Maurice and Maralyn were known as loners. When they

weren't at their jobs, they laboured on the boat, every weekend, every evening. They rarely went out. "Good seamanship begins in port with the most perfect and detailed preparations that it is possible to make," wrote Hiscock. Maurice took the instruction seriously. He strengthened the hull, modified the fore rigging for trade wind sailing, overhauled the engine and electrical fittings, redesigned and rebuilt the galley and toilet, put in extra fuel and water tanks and lockers. Each part had to be faultless.

At the tax office, Maralyn made a new friend, June, a tiny, round-faced woman who liked to chat. Maralyn invited June and her fiancé, Colin Foskett, down to the boat for a drink one evening. Colin, a sandy-haired carpenter, was as cheerful as his wife. Maralyn felt she had to warn them in advance: Maurice was different. He might be odd. He might like you, he might not, but he'll be awkward either way.

Colin and June didn't mind. Yes, Maurice could be graceless in company, gauche and blunt, but they were the kinds of people who could find common ground with anyone and they liked Maralyn enough to tolerate her husband. Maurice enjoyed going out for dinner and introducing them to wine. They invited Maurice and Maralyn to their wedding. Maurice said no.

Over the years, the Fosketts regularly came to help on the boat. Colin would arrive at the boatyard on his motorbike, wearing leathers, smoking a cigarette. Maurice didn't smoke. Colin found Maurice to be strange about his woodwork, the way he'd do a job over and over until he was sure it was perfect.

In return for their help, Maurice and Maralyn took Colin and June on some of their practice voyages along the coast and across the Channel to Normandy. The trips allowed them to establish their roles on board. Every crew, even a crew of two, requires a hierarchy. Maurice was captain, navigator, and mechanic. Maralyn was in charge of provisions and the galley. When Colin and June came along, Colin was the handyman and June was given the role of the bosun, a title dating from the eleventh century that refers to the crew member in charge of the deck. Maurice, an admirer of ancient sailing vernacular, insisted on calling her the bosun at all times, on and off shore. If everyone on board knew their job, and what was expected of them, there would be no confusion about what needed doing or how it should be done.

It made for a funny kind of freedom. Their boat, like all successful boats, was a form of benign autocracy that depended on inflexible rules. There is almost nothing as rigid and conformist as the systems on board a boat. You have to conform to survive.

Maralyn adapted to the regime naturally. Through her preparations, she came to know the exact quantities of food required before a voyage, both tinned and fresh, to last them until the next port when they would restock at a shop. A thirty-foot yacht, she calculated, should be capable of stowing five hundred cans of food: meats, soups, vegetables, fruits, drinks, powdered and evaporated milk. Maralyn removed each can's paper label, marked it with a code to indicate its contents ("a black felt pen is adequate for this job"), and then treated the top and bottom with a clear varnish to protect it from damp and rust. Fresh fruits were individually wrapped in newspaper and turned regularly to avoid bruising. Over time, she developed formulas for the exact quantity of ingredients required per person per day. Eggs: 1 per person per day, plus 4 a week for cooking. Sugar: 1

ounce per person per day, and 1¾ pounds per person for cooking. Cheese: 1 ounce per person per day. Milk: ¼ pint per person per day. Biscuits or crackers: 1 packet a day alternating between savoury and sweet. "Allow a contingency of 15 per cent (possibly savoury only)."

Maurice tended to make a mess of the kitchen. Everything worked best when they had total control over their separate domains. Only Maurice's creeping insecurity sometimes got in the way, when he wasn't quite able to maintain the unflinching self-confidence required of the person in charge. If he ever asked Maralyn for reassurance about their route, she'd remind him sharply that navigation was his department. "She was right, of course." She had a habit of being right.

~

Auralyn needed testing, and so did they. It wasn't enough to plot your passage and build your boat, wrote Hiscock. You had to prepare *yourself.*

Somehow this didn't quite extend to Maralyn learning to swim. A sailing friend tried to teach her, but Maralyn was afraid to enter the water. She knew how to sail, trusted in Maurice, and if something went wrong, so be it. Maurice tried to encourage her, but it was very hard to make Maralyn do something she didn't want to do. She reasoned that if it came to it, and the choice was between drowning and swimming to safety, she'd probably manage.

Anyway, it all seemed unlikely. She was on a boat, wasn't she, and that required its own training. "Manning a sailing boat,"

Maurice wrote with the relish a certain kind of person feels for self-denial and physical hardship, "demands a total commitment to the unrelenting austerity and discomfort for the wet and cramped conditions on board." They had to get used to bad weather, broken sleep, and bouts of seasickness that could render a person incapable for days.

And solitude. For days and weeks, crossing oceans, they would be alone. You might see only one ship a month, warned Hiscock. In other words, don't expect help if something goes wrong. If someone is hurt, if you run out of water or a crew member becomes unwell, you will have only yourselves.

For Maurice, it was like a commandment. They had to be self-reliant. Weakness was not an option. They had to be ready for every imaginable disaster. A friend taught him how to fish out at sea in Christchurch Bay. He studied how to extract plankton from seawater. They decided to take a lemon squeezer with them, which could be used to wring drinkable water out of the raw flesh of fish.

Every sailor feels anxious before a voyage, assured Hiscock, but a good one will have prepared so tirelessly that they will no longer be plagued by self-doubt. But what if you were someone who had only ever felt self-doubt? Maurice could do the fixing and the checking, the lists, but seamanship, *good* seamanship, seemed to involve something else. Something you couldn't prepare for in advance, or learn from a book.

In a long passage on the importance of vigilance, Hiscock chastised himself for the time he nearly wrecked his boat when he failed to check the location of a light as he approached the Panama shore. It was his own fault. His approach had been "unseamanlike." There was simply nothing worse, on a boat, than a captain being unseamanlike. It was like an army officer betraying cowardice.

So how did you become seamanlike, this elusive, essential quality? Yes, it would accrue through experience, Maurice knew, and involved skill, learning, and a commonsense intelligence. But there also seemed to be something more fundamental at play: It appeared to reflect character. In a crisis at sea, there isn't time to ponder or deliberate. You can't be defeatist. Things go wrong, and even great sailors make mistakes. People get tired or overconfident. Their judgement skews. You have to adapt. You need to know what to do and how to do it in an instant; to act with a kind of light, unthinking instinct, the way a dancer might shift position mid-flight. It sounded, worryingly for Maurice, close to an art.

FOUR

In June 1972, England was cold and wet. Along parts of the south coast, the entire month passed in gloom. Falmouth claimed the record: the coldest June since 1869.

Maurice and Maralyn had been waiting for a turn in the conditions, a fair wind and warm sun that would open up the sky like a blessing. But it didn't come. They had to reach the Canary Islands in time to catch the trade winds that would carry them across the Atlantic, but the foul, squally days showed no sign of passing.

Early on 28 June, the sky still dark and clouded, Colin and June came to see them off from their moorings on the Hamble. Maurice hugged the bosun. June handed Maralyn a box of homemade cakes. The men shook hands. Maurice felt a sudden surge of emotion, the kind he was never quite sure what to do with.

Only seagulls were there to witness the farewell, circling and squawking. Maurice cast off the last mooring line, and they sailed into the tidal stream.

As *Auralyn* moved out into the choppy grey waters of the Solent, the sky began to lighten at its edges. Maurice sailed as slowly as he could, wanting to remember the moment, which was surely the most significant of his life. He looked back at the village of Bursledon on the hillside, the redbrick cottages with white sash windows, the trees in full leaf silhouetted black against the sky. He'd never see any of it again.

Departure is always clarifying, but particularly so on a boat. One moment, you are bound to the land by a rope; the next you are not. You are attached to a nation and its people; then you loosen the tie. Emigration contains two forces: the pull of what you are going towards, or what you imagine you are going towards, and the release from what you are leaving behind, or what you imagine you are leaving behind.

As they sailed away, it seemed clear that their old life was ending and their new life beginning. He was free.

~

The sea was rough and frothy as they crossed Lyme Bay. Maurice went below deck to fix a leaking valve in the freshwater system. When he came back up, he found Maralyn sitting in the cockpit, sobbing. It was the Devon cliffs in the distance, she said. A last sight of England. There is nothing like seeing a place for the last time to erase its imperfections.

The demands of the boat took over soon enough. Maralyn busied herself with chores. "She quickly perked up," wrote Maurice.

At Falmouth, they waited for the north wind that would carry them across the Bay of Biscay to Spain. To pass the time, they dismantled and reassembled equipment, checked ropes and sails, re-stowed all the lockers. All things they'd already done, over and over.

Every day they went to the harbourmaster's office to study the weather forecasts, set out in detailed reports of the atmospheric conditions and moving patterns of high or low pressure. Eventually, Maurice spotted an anticyclone building in the northwest of Ireland. It was the sign he'd been waiting for. They left the next day.

Crossing the bay, notorious for its bad weather and heaving seas, they were out of sight of land for the first time. Maurice felt a release, like a long-taut muscle unclenching. Sailing was always liberating, but there was a gut difference between sailing along a coast, its towns and hills in sight, and sailing out on the open sea where there was no longer any visible evidence of other people, as if they might never have existed in the first place. Everything beyond themselves had gone.

~

Five days at sea and they reached Spain's Galician coast, invisible in fog. They anchored at the port of Viveiro, whose ancient walls had once withstood pirates and enclosed plagues. Then they sailed gradually south: Cedeira, Ferrol, A Coruña, Camariñas, around Cape Finisterre, Corcubión, Muros, Arousa, Pontevedra, past the Islas Cíes, finally to Baiona, where the harbour is overlooked by a fortress.

At the Baiona yacht club they showered and collected fuel and water. The marina was busy, boats jostling next to each other. They met their neighbours, an English couple called Brian and Sue, also childless and planning to cross the Atlantic; meaningful coincidences.

They ate dinner on each other's boats. Even Maurice enjoyed himself despite Brian being another species of man, muscly and agile, at home in his body and the world, the kind of person who could easily have made Maurice feel inadequate. But socialising was different on water: Everyone was a fellow sailor, always moving on, obsessed with boats. There was ready-made conversation: comparing gear, provisions, weather. And Maurice was good at this conversation, fluent in its language. He was good at sailing. It gave him a feeling of competence. He often found himself helping others he judged to be woefully underprepared.

They followed Brian and Sue to Cascais, Portugal, then to the island of Madeira, seven hundred miles away in the Atlantic. Just before midnight they saw the lights of Funchal harbour winking and heard a shout in the darkness. There was Brian, in his dinghy, guiding them to anchor.

The four explored the island, its pine forests and mountains, falling streams and Portuguese houses. They went walking in the hills and visited a monastery. "I cannot remember if it was an active cloistered community but it served us excellent tea and cakes," noted Maurice. They ran down the island's steep cobbled roads holding hands.

One afternoon, the barometer dropped, a sudden loss of air pressure. Black clouds raced across the sky. They had just enough time to prepare: checking the anchors and putting out the fenders, like floating bumpers, to protect the boat. They laid out their emergency equipment and waterproofs, just in case. They'd never seen rain like it. As the storm set in, the wind was so strong the anemometer could no longer read its speed. Lightning lit up the coast and they saw neighbouring boats straining at their anchor chains. Maurice heard a roar rising above the noise of the weather, then saw a wall of water burst through the channel into the harbour, carrying boulders from the hills. Maralyn thought she spotted a cow in the torrent. A motor launch broke free of its mooring and began ricocheting among the boats like a pinball. Maurice towed it until he could secure it to a mooring and on his way gave a lift to a young German couple who wanted to get out of the storm and spend the night in a hotel. Maurice, unperturbed by the weather, felt no need to follow their lead. Once he'd dropped them off, he returned to Maralyn and they stayed up all night, listening to the storm as it raged.

The next day they spent hours untangling anchors. Madeira, Maurice decided, "had lost some of its charm." They sailed away, towards the Canary Islands, in an afternoon haze.

Five days later, Maralyn rushed below deck. Maurice, bent over his chart, was plotting their position. She pulled him up on deck and pointed to the horizon where they could see the peak of Mount Teide, Tenerife's twelve-thousand-foot volcano, poking through a perfect ring of white cloud. "With a degree of flippancy," wrote Maurice, "Maralyn asked why spend time working out our position when there was such a distinctive target to aim for sitting squarely on the horizon?" Maurice just needed to lift his head up and look.

~

In Tenerife, they met other ocean crossers, all waiting for their moment. Brian and Sue again; a couple called Nevil and Sheila and their two young sons; and Anne and David, "a lute player of international acclaim." Maurice regretted having little knowledge of the lute, or its repertoire.

One morning, at breakfast, Brian knocked on their hull. "They're here!" he said. The trade winds. Maurice shaved. There was a last supper at the lutenist's hotel that Maurice attended in his socks after pulling a full shopping trolley over his foot in the supermarket and breaking his toe.

The next morning, they sailed out of La Palma's harbour alongside Brian and Sue, the two couples calling out to each other as their boats cut through the water. By the following dawn, their friends had disappeared from view. So had everything else. Any ship with an engine had no use for the trade winds and could take a more direct route across the ocean. They saw no boats, no planes, nothing at all.

Maurice slipped into an almost sublime state. The ports, with their yacht clubs and chatter and bustle, were distracting for a while, but the great release of ocean sailing, the severance from land and its inhabitants, was what he'd always craved. From horizon to horizon lay an unbroken body of water and an open sky. "We were happy with our isolation," he wrote, "and at peace with everyone and the world."

~

The crossing from the Canaries to the Caribbean took them twenty-four days. Twenty-seven hundred miles of ocean. Maurice liked to say that he and Maralyn sailed "by the seat of their pants," but in reality his methods were highly technical and dependent on a collection of instruments.

Maurice had a compass, a log, a small revolving mechanism that trailed in the water and measured the speed they were travelling, and an anemometer, "our only concession to electronic gadgetry," which measured the local wind speeds. Most important, he had a sextant, a handheld telescope-like instrument that sailors have used to navigate by the stars since the eighteenth century. The sextant measures the distance between two objects, typically the horizon and the sun or moon or stars. In the evenings, Maurice and Maralyn would plot which stars they'd use, picking five bright ones at as wide an angle as possible. Then, at dawn or dusk, when both stars and the horizon were visible, Maurice would look through the telescope of the sextant and "take the sight," noting the time on his chronometer, an exact, maritime timepiece. With this information, and referring to his *Nautical Almanac*, which listed the position of the celestial bodies for every hour of the year, Maurice could then work out where they were on his charts.

Maurice revelled in this work. He loved the numbers and

diagrams, the process of computation. He'd read Cook's journals, full of his workings, each measurement precise to the minute or second. "For us the boundless ocean stretched to four horizons but I was always amazed and satisfied that I knew on which part of it we belonged," he wrote. Boundlessness was all very well, but he could contain it in a sum.

~

The twenty-four days followed a rhythm, set by the sun. Breakfast at dawn, then work, clearing the deck of flying fish, which littered the boat as if they'd rained from the sky during the night. The morning always presented an urgent task: a chafing sail, sediment in the fuel tank, a deck leak.

In the afternoon, in the heat of the day, they rested, played chess, read. Every spare shelf was loaded with books, exchanged for new material at yacht clubs on their way. Maralyn sewed, embroidering their pile of signal flags and courtesy ensigns, flown when entering foreign harbours.

At sunset, they prepared the boat for the night. Maralyn cooked, and they ate dinner. Once it was dark again, the sky patterned with stars, they extinguished all the lights on board apart from a single oil lamp. They tried to make as little sound as possible while on watch, so as not to disturb the other's sleep.

Every day was hot, faultless. Open skies and light winds. They stopped wearing anything, including life jackets. There didn't seem much point.

It rained three times, their only chance to wash. When they saw the clouds gather, they quickly soaped themselves and stood beneath the shower of rain hoping it would last long enough to rinse the lather from their bodies.

They saw almost nothing, apart from the flying fish and a school of dolphins that appeared to be standing on their tails, as if putting on a show.

No whales, though. In his diaries, Cook had recorded encounters with wildlife, including numerous whales. In doing so, he had caused "a holocaust in centuries to come," Maurice wrote, by revealing to whalers the location of their prey. The ocean would once have been teeming with their vast, slick bodies, roaming in pods. Now there was no sign of them at all.

~

Land! The birds gave it away, circling and swooping as they hunted for fish in the warmer waters of the Caribbean. Frigate birds, boobies, bosun birds, petrels with their white bottoms skating across the water: ambassadors from the coast.

Maurice saw a blinking dot of light in the distance: the lighthouse on the eastern cape of Barbados. Elated, he stayed up all night to follow it and let Maralyn sleep, taking fixes to ensure he steered a course to the southernmost point of the island.

At dawn, he saw waving rows of palm trees and green fields stretching up behind. Fishermen were already out on their boats. Maurice went down to wake Maralyn, who jumped out of her bunk, naked, and ran straight up on deck. She stood in front of the fishermen, still naked, and shouted, "But it's just like England!"

They sailed into the clear turquoise water of Carlisle Bay, a perfect strip of golden sand bordered by palm trees. Not quite England, apart from its colonial name, taken from Barbados's former "lord proprietor," the Earl of Carlisle. Perhaps it was the sight of trees after so long at sea.

Their friends' boats were already there. Nevil, Sheila, and the boys clambered over to visit them first, bearing a loaf of bread and eggs. Brian and Sue came for dinner in the evening. Maurice fetched a bottle of Asti Spumante that they'd saved for the occasion and toasted their triumph. They had crossed an ocean.

Later, after their guests had returned to their boats, Maurice and Maralyn stayed on deck in the darkness, holding each other. The shore lights flickered in the distance. They couldn't sleep, fired by what they had just done, which seemed extraordinary, even though they knew it had been done many times before. The wilderness of an ocean can have that effect. It feels possible that you might have been the first.

"Strangely," wrote Maurice, whose mind had a tendency to get in the way of uncomplicated joy, "now that it was all over, it was difficult to sit back and gain perspective."

~

Tall palms and mangrove forests, scarlet hibiscus and white frangipani. Eddies of warm air. After the great grey plain of the ocean, the Caribbean was a rush of colour and scent. They sheltered in bays, the boat shifting softly on the clear water, the reefs alive with fish.

In 1972, the islands were still relatively undeveloped. Maurice knew it couldn't last. Barbados had become independent of

British colonial rule six years earlier, and Errol Barrow, the prime minister, wanted to reduce his country's dependence on exports from sugar plantations, staffed for years by enslaved Africans shipped over by the British. In his vision, the new economy would be fuelled by tourism. The package holidays now popular in Europe would find their way here, Maurice was sure. "Where we walked among palm trees, we found ourselves picturing garish hotels springing up," he wrote, capable of spoiling even paradise with his imagination, "their noisy clientele crowding the beach, bodies oiled and glistening in the sun."

In the afternoons, their sailing friends started going to the Barbados Yacht Club, which had only recently dropped the "Royal" from its title. The club served tea and buttered toast, as if it were a tearoom in the Home Counties. Maurice, ashamed of his country's colonial past, objected to the place in principle. The instinct to colonise struck him, like whaling, as another example of human cruelty and idiocy. "Exploitation of other races in the name of 'God and king' was a piece of impudent and blasphemous nonsense," he wrote.

But their friends liked the club, and the tea and buttered toast were free. Maurice, for once relishing social interaction, found his principles slipping and went along too. Most days, he sat at a table under a palm tree in front of the clubhouse and debated the existence of God with Brian and a Swiss priest called Walter. Their wives didn't contribute, Maurice noted, but listened to the discussion attentively, if "sometimes nettled—particularly Maralyn—by our entrenched postulations."

But these were golden days. New friends, vigorous conversation, picnics on land, dinners on board. On the dock one day,

Maurice met a local fisherman called Rudy who invited them to a party at his house. They dressed up in their best things, rowed to shore in the dinghy, and walked to Rudy's house, which was already packed with guests. "It would be quite inappropriate for me to judge the success or otherwise of a party since socialising is not a natural predisposition of mine," wrote Maurice, having a go anyway, "but from the number of people present and the noise, it seemed as though it must have been a triumph."

Maurice talked to his fellow guests as best he could, then retreated to the kitchen to help Rudy's wife do the washing up. Later, someone suggested he check on Maralyn. He found her lying on a sofa—"drunk as a lord!" on neat rum.

Maurice manoeuvred her into a taxi, but she was unconscious by the time they got to the beach. He dragged her across the sand to the dinghy, rowed back to *Auralyn*, pulled her over the side, and wrangled her down the ladder into the cabin. "There were to be many other parties," wrote Maurice, "but Maralyn had learned her lesson."

~

The weeks passed quickly; days made indistinguishable by pleasure. Apparently, it was nearly Christmas, not that Christmas meant much to them. On Union Island, they anchored in a blue-water lagoon next to Nevil and Sheila and their boys. Maurice swam in the afternoons; they played Scrabble in the evenings.

On Christmas morning, Maurice took the boys snorkelling. He heard a splash, and looked up to see two naked women swimming nearby. "By any measure, the most enjoyable Christmas treat I could ever remember."

Maurice worried about the boys, though. Should he get them out of the water, give them a little talk? It didn't come easily, to be so forward. "We continued to swim as if nothing had happened and later I told no one."

That evening, they gathered on Nevil and Sheila's boat for Christmas dinner. Nevil had rigged up some fairy lights and got hold of a tree. They pulled crackers and drank homemade ginger beer that he and Sheila had brought all the way from home. One of the bottles exploded all over them.

On to Bequia, then St. Vincent. Maralyn made drop scones. St. Lucia and Martinique. She saw a horse run along a beach and made sausage rolls. Dominica and Guadeloupe. They hosted a dinner: steak, sausage, roast potatoes, rum punch.

"Nice to meet everyone again," Maralyn wrote in her diary. She spent her days shopping and cooking, a constant round of entertaining or being entertained.

In Antigua, they went to a steel band concert. Someone pinched Sue's bottom and she told the others, enraged. She considered the act a sexual assault. Maralyn agreed. Maurice, not quite caught up with the decade's fresh feminist energy, found their accusations disproportionate to the crime. He attempted some jokes, which were ignored. Then he reached behind Brian, who was standing next to Maralyn, and pinched Maralyn's bottom. He knew, immediately, that he'd made a mistake. Maurice's idea of what might be funny was not always shared by other people. Maralyn hit Brian, assuming he was the pincher. Maurice had to jump in to explain. Maralyn, mortified, apologised to Brian, then turned to her husband. "There was a look in her eyes," wrote Maurice, "that told me it was not going to be a good idea for me to be alone in her company for some little time to come."

~

The parties had to stop eventually. The year turned and they moved on; the schedule demanded it. You can't cross the Pacific on a whim. Maurice got a bad cold.

"Maurice still snuffling," Maralyn noted in her diary on 24 January 1973. Maurice's colds tended to last.

A week later, they sailed out of Antigua's English Harbour. Their ten-day voyage to Panama was hit by violent storms. A giant wave crashed over the boat and bent one of the crosstrees, a horizontal beam in the rigging, halfway up the mast. Maralyn, repeatedly sick, tried to reassure Maurice. Worse had happened to them already; doubtless worse would happen again.

During the long, "lumpy" nights, as Maralyn described them, the boat took on water. On the morning of 7 February, she counted twenty-seven flying fish strewn across the deck and in the cockpit. "A cat's feast!" she wrote. One, to her amazement, had dived through the hatch and down into the bilge.

They arrived in the port of Cristóbal, gateway to the Panama Canal, in the rain. The canal, fifty miles long, would take only around twelve hours to pass through, and cost them dues of $8.47, but it was a logistical puzzle. To get through the locks, the boat needed to be attached to four eighty-foot lines with extra crew to handle the ropes. Either they hired the crew at great expense, or they found fellow transient sailors to help them for free and they offered the same service in return. After they waited a week, a Belgian yacht turned up crewed by two brothers, Jean and Jacques, who agreed to the exchange.

Early in the morning, they followed a large container ship into the canal's first vast chamber, 1,000 feet long, 110 feet wide. Too small to navigate the canal alone, they had to tag along behind a major vessel. *Auralyn* looked like a small dog, easily stepped on, trotting after its master. Stevedores threw down the lines, which they attached to their ropes on board in order to keep the boat central in the chamber. The lock gates closed behind them, and the lock began to fill with a surge of water through the culverts. Maurice, frantic as he made sure the ropes were taut, hardly noticed the water rising beneath them, lifting the boat. On they went, through Gatun Lake and Pedro Miguel Lock, until they reached the final lock at Miraflores, where the freshwater of the canal meets the salt water of the Pacific Ocean and the sea convulses.

The Pacific, at last. "Alluring, boundless, to us unknown," wrote Maurice. "Our *terra incognita*."

In Balboa, they took the boat apart and put it back together again. They checked and double-checked the emergency bag and re-stowed the lockers. Maralyn varnished surfaces, mended her sleeping bag, repainted the cabin roof, stocked up at the supermarket, and wrote letters home, including a nautical quiz for June. Four days were spent antifouling the boat, repainting the hull to protect it from algae and barnacles. Maurice found the job arduous, always worried that he might not have the right kinds of brushes or enough time to do it properly.

"With constellations of sunken volcanoes and atolls of coral reefs stretching before us on a vast universe of sea," he wrote, tilting between high feeling and anxiety, "we were very conscious that all our preparations had to be thorough."

~

At first light on 26 February 1973, nearly eight months after leaving England, they began the first stage of their Pacific crossing, from Balboa to the Galápagos. A gentle wind blew—the start of the southeast trade winds. Maurice estimated it was about 960 nautical miles and ten days sailing until they reached the Galápagos.

The ocean was calm. Dolphins swam around the boat. In the early hours of the morning, Maralyn noted, their long milky wakes looked like snakes in the phosphorescence.

As the day grew light, the sun glinting off the water, Maurice thought the Pacific was living up to its name. Tranquil, clear, and blue, the water stretched to the horizon under a cloudless sky.

The Atlantic had been a trial run, its cold waters familiar, but the Pacific was of a different order: a wilderness so vast that storms gather and disperse unseen. Far beneath the surface, where it is darker than any darkness known on land, debris from decomposing organisms sinks to the floor, and it looks as though it were constantly snowing. The average depth of the ocean is thirteen thousand feet. The Mariana Trench in the western Pacific, at 36,000 below the surface, is the deepest point on the planet. According to the few who have descended, the seabed there is a kind of gelatinous ooze.

It can seem like a desert, this ocean, featureless and empty. But deep down, there is landscape, peaks and valleys, whole mountain ranges. There are whales sleeping vertically with their calves, or clicking messages to each other as they search for squid. Baby turtles swim out into the open ocean, their flippers pumping back and forth.

Auralyn carved her path. Above them, the sun bore down. They rigged up a green awning over the cockpit for shelter, but Maralyn still managed to get sunburnt on her chest. To pass the long white days, she crocheted and wrote in her diary, noting what they saw. There wasn't much to write. "No shipping—no fish." *Auralyn* was marking a single line, thin and straight, across one of the vacant spaces on the map. On 3 March, Maurice took the sights. "M estimates only 325 miles to go," wrote Maralyn. At their usual rate of around 100 miles a day, that meant three days sailing until they reached the Galápagos. Nothing, really.

FIVE

At three o'clock in the morning, on 4 March, they quietly swapped over the watch. During the night, the ocean appeared only as shifting planes of blackness. All at once it was alight. They were passing a fishing boat, blazing like a funfair in a dark field. The first sign of fellow human life in six days.

A searchlight from the boat scanned the water, illuminating the surface with circles of white. Dinghies moved around the boat's edges as if looking for something dropped in the ocean. Briefly the searchlight moved over them, the small world of *Auralyn* caught in its glare: Maralyn, short and slight; Maurice, taller and stooped, hair thinning on the top of his head.

Seeing the fishing boat was a fleeting shock, like noticing a figure passing across a window in a remote house. It was unnerving to see people and movement, something alive when they didn't expect it, but they forgot the encounter soon enough. It's one of the liberations of sailing. Everything recedes. You are always moving into new waters, new weather. Whatever you pass disappears.

~

At dawn, Maralyn came below deck. The sun had risen, the edge of the waves catching the day's new light. She turned on the stove, then went to rouse Maurice, touching his shoulder.

When the crash came, sending the books flying, they felt the violence in their bodies. Maurice was up the ladder in a second, moving the way people do in crisis, without knowledge of movement. Up on deck, the boom was swinging free and the sails flapping hopelessly like white sheets on a washing line.

There was the whale, thrashing, its blood pouring into the ocean. A suspended moment, as they watched it wrestle with its pain. Then the frenzy as they pumped and shouted, scrambled to cover the hole or stuff it, anything to stop the water from filling the boat. The decision to abandon ship was taken in a moment: a look exchanged. There was no one they could tell, of course, having no radio transmitter.

After that, it was pragmatism, executed quietly. The life raft unleashed; the dinghy inflated. Water containers gathered. Anything else they could salvage from the flooded cabin crammed into bags: tins of food, pencils and passports, logbooks and diaries, as if they knew their words would outlive them.

Maralyn took photographs as their boat slowly sank. They didn't say a word, numbed by the unfolding loss. Years of work, a vessel they loved like a child, was disappearing beneath the surface, tilting as she went. She didn't even look particularly damaged, only askew and abandoned.

She might still be down there now. Bits of her, anyway. The wood will have rotted, the metal rusted. Salt corrodes. Bacteria, fish, crustaceans, and molluscs will have consumed what it is possible to consume. But there'll be parts still there, small indestructible objects. She will have become her own ecosystem, deep-ocean creatures living among her remains.

It's thought that there are around three million shipwrecks at the bottom of the sea, a shadow world, mostly unexplored. In 1628, the *Vasa*, a Swedish warship, sank a mile offshore on her maiden voyage in the first strong wind she ever encountered. When she was salvaged three centuries later, in 1961, her hull was still largely intact. Marine archaeologists found clothes and coins, cutlery and tools.

The *Titanic*, on the other hand, will soon disappear completely. They can't bring her up: too deep, too hard. In 1986, during the first manned expedition to her wreck 12,500 feet down on the floor of the Atlantic, a deep-sea robot took pictures of shoes lying side by side, still intact thanks to the tannin in the leather. Each pair marked the final resting place of a body, long ago lost to the water.

Part Two

ONE

They floated separately. Maralyn in the life raft, Maurice in the dinghy. Neither spoke. The silence, apart from the pattering of the waves, seemed to have its own weight.

Maralyn tied the things they'd saved around the edge of the raft. If in doubt, do. Things always need to be done. All vessels, all homes, however small and insubstantial, require a system.

The walls of the raft, four feet six inches in diameter, were formed of two inflated rings. The floor was a single layer of rubber-proofed material. A third semicircular tube arched from one side of the top tube to the other and supported a bright orange canopy. Altogether, it resembled a sort of floating tent. On one side was its entrance, covered by a flap, and on the other side was a ventilation duct and a small lookout window, protected by another flap of material.

Inside, along one edge, Maralyn placed the sail bag packed

with clothes, a plastic box containing their navigation books, and a one-gallon plastic water container. Along the opposite side she put another water container, a box containing the sextant, a plastic bowl full of cans of food, the Campingaz butane stove, and an empty plastic bucket for catching water. She left a small space in the middle for them to sit, facing each other. They wouldn't have room to lie down.

Around them floated items that had sprung from *Auralyn* as she sank. Maurice, rowing the dinghy, retrieved what he could: four containers of water, one of kerosene, one of methylated spirits, a jar of Coffee-Mate, a tin of margarine, two pencils. Her last offerings.

After it was all stowed, he attached the dinghy to the raft with two twenty-five-foot lines, a straightforward task that seemed to take him an exceptionally long time, rowing backwards and forwards between the two. His body appeared to have forgotten what to do. At last, the two craft, like prisoners, were tied together.

Maurice rested for a moment. He looked across at Maralyn and saw that she was weeping.

~

When a boat sinks, it is the captain's fault. There is no one else to blame. Captaincy, like any leadership, is a series of decisions, and he'd made the wrong ones. It was quite clear.

Think of all the things he could have done differently! They could have left a day later from Panama. Taken a more southerly course. They might never have met the whale. Even if they had, surely there had been a way of saving the boat. They'd had time, after all, forty minutes from the strike of the whale until she started to sink. Had they given up pumping too soon? Perhaps if they'd gone on stuffing the hole, they could have stabilised her long enough to get the water out. She'd been their home, their future, and he'd just watched her go down, helpless. It was his failure, as total and personal as any he'd known. Someone else, someone better, would have known what to do.

Maralyn persuaded Maurice to come and sit with her in the raft. The canopy would at least shelter them from the burn of the sun once it was at its height. Facing each other, legs aligned like pencils in a tin, they went over what had happened. What about that fishing boat they'd passed when they swapped over the watch? Perhaps it had been a whaling ship. Perhaps those little boats and the searchlight had been looking for a whale they'd harpooned but failed to catch. Perhaps the whale had escaped, injured and angry, followed them for the rest of the night, and collided with them in some sort of misguided revenge attack. It was only a theory, but somehow it was more comforting than the idea that it was all pure coincidence, pure misfortune. That their boat had sunk for no reason at all.

They considered their chances. Maurice, being honest, thought they were doomed but didn't say so. He told Maralyn they were near a shipping lane, which was true, and that they'd probably be seen soon, which wasn't. The only ship they'd encountered on the Pacific so far had been that fishing boat. Remember Hiscock: You might see only one ship a month, and it was hardly likely another would pass close enough to the raft to spot them.

Maralyn wondered if the various friends they were due to

meet in the Galápagos would raise the alarm. Someone would notice that they hadn't arrived. But this happens all the time, Maurice knew. You say you'll meet at the next port, but your paths don't cross. Someone takes another route, or changes their plans; the weather intervenes. Even if the alarm were raised, what would be the point? How do you search for two people in the middle of an ocean?

They had no radio transmitter, no motor. No way of telling anyone what had happened, or of getting anywhere. Their two small, inflatable craft would be impossible to spot in the vast expanse of water. Like cargo that fell off the back of a container ship, no one would know they were missing until they washed up on a coast thousands of miles away.

Sailing had given Maurice such a feeling of control, such agency. For months he had been harnessing the elements, using them as fuel. He'd raced across the seas as if he were their master. Now the wind could buffet them wherever it chose.

TWO

Establish a routine. Maintain order. Don't let the structures dissolve. Maralyn knew all this in her soul.

After she'd cried, Maralyn turned to what needed doing. It was morning. Morning meant breakfast. She spread some biscuits with margarine and a thin layer of marmalade and they ate in silence.

They'd get hungry fast, thought Maurice, if this was what their meals were going to be like.

Then what. There was, Maurice realised, very little to do, a state at odds with everything he associated with being at sea. The day, like the ocean, opened out around them, empty and formless. "What on earth can we do to keep ourselves occupied?" he asked.

Maralyn told him which books she'd salvaged, the Hiscock and a biography of Richard III. Maurice groaned. The life of a fifteenth-century king didn't seem relevant, and he'd read the Hiscock endlessly. In any case, what use was a practical guide to circumnavigating the globe when their boat was at the bottom of the ocean? Hiscock's sermons on seamanship would read like taunts now.

Maralyn was insistent. They could use the books as the basis for a library when they got home. Maurice felt a surge of frustration. Surely she could see there was barely enough room for food, let alone books?

"Never mind," said Maralyn. "We can read them and analyse them line by line and discuss them."

He knew she was right. They'd need stimulation to occupy their minds. Keeping busy was essential. Look at Maralyn: organising, tidying, housekeeping the raft as if it were their living room in the Allestree bungalow. Doing limited the dangers of thinking.

Everything they owned in the world was now arranged around them on less than five feet of raft. Maralyn compiled an inventory.

2 Blue bowls

1 Round bucket

1 Oblong bucket

1 Plastic wastepaper basket

2 Cushions

2 Towels

1 Camera

2 Sail bags

2 Oilskin jackets and trousers

1 Binoculars

1 Tilley lamp

1 Mallet

1 Sextant

1 Compass

2 Books

2 Dictionaries

1 Camping Gaz stove

1 Torch

1 Scissors

1 Pliers

2 Plates

2 Mugs

2 Saucepans (small)

1 Bag clothes

1 Deck-watch

Navigation books

Ship's papers and Log

2 Diaries

Mariner's knife and marline spike

1 Box safety matches

2 Pencils

1 Felt pen (found in Maralyn's oilskin pocket)

Emergency bag: First-aid kit, knife, fork and spoon each, penknife, small walking compass, vitamin tablets, glucose, Heinz baby food, nuts, dates, peanuts, water bottles

Then she wrote another list, of their remaining food.

2 tins	*Steak and kidney pie filling*
1 tin	*Ambrosia rice pudding*
2 tins	*Fray Bentos steak and kidney pudding*
2 tins	*Tyne Brand minced beef*
2 tins	*Wall's braised steak*
1 tin	*Sainsbury's ravioli*
1 tin	*Curry*
3 tins	*Sardines*
1 tin	*Wall's pork luncheon meat*
1 tin	*Ham and egg roll*
6 tins	*Campbell's spaghetti bolognaise*
1 tin	*Blue Band margarine*
2 tins	*Carnation evaporated milk*
2 tins	*Carnation condensed milk*
1 tin	*Tate & Lyle treacle*
1 tin	*Big-D peanuts*
4 tins	*Heinz baby foods*
1 pkt	*Whitworth's brazil nuts*

½ packet	*Dates*
1 bottle	*Boots Multivite vitamin tablets*
½ jar	*Carnation Coffee-Mate*
½ jar	*Robertson's marmalade*
4 pkts	*Carr's biscuits*
½ sm. jar	*Boots glucose powder*
1	*Huntley & Palmers Dundee cake*

It wasn't much. Thirty-three tins, a few dates and nuts. One Dundee cake, packed for her birthday on 24 April. Surely they'd be rescued by then and could get another cake. The cake, like everything else, would have to be eaten as slowly as possible, in daily slivers. The water ration, meanwhile, was a single pint a day taken from the containers in the dinghy. One cup at breakfast, with three spoonfuls of Coffee-Mate, then more at lunch and dinner. Until it rained and they found a way of catching it, they would have to make their limited supply last.

Maralyn wrote out a timetable, calculating their daily allowance.

(7:30am) B/Fast piece of Dundee + margarine

Cup water (between 2)

10am 1 Butterscotch sweet

Lunch 12 Midday Few peanuts one date each one ginger bisc each 1 cup water x 2

Dinner 6pm 1 tin meat x 2 1 cup water

If they were strict, she estimated that they could stretch the food to last for about twenty days, which sounded like a very long time to be stuck on a raft in the middle of an ocean.

Still, Maralyn was optimistic. She knew the Galápagos were close. Maurice, who knew more about the winds and currents, didn't tell her how unlikely it was that they'd be blown in the right direction. He found himself wondering if they had enough gas in the canister to kill themselves.

~

It would help, at least, to know where they were. Using his compass and chart, Maurice estimated that they were 250 miles north of Ecuador and 300 miles east of the Galápagos. If he was right, that meant they were close to a shipping lane but too far north for the current to carry them west towards the islands. The southeasterly wind would drive them even farther north. If they drifted around 25 miles a day, it would take about twelve days to reach the longitude of the Galápagos. But how could they get down to them?

The dinghy had oars, he thought. They could row. If they took turns rowing south for ten miles a day, they would eventually reach the islands' latitude. He wasn't sure they were capable of rowing ten miles a day with the raft in tow. Perhaps they should cut it off. But the dinghy had no shelter. And what if it sank? They'd have no backup. Why did every problem seem to contain more problems?

He no longer felt able to make a decision. Maralyn would know what to do.

After lunch, a handful of peanuts each, he mentioned the

idea. Maralyn was immediately convinced. "We'll have to do the rowing at night," she said. "It would be impossible in the heat of the day." If it was too dark to see the compass, they could steer by the stars. They'd start that evening, she said, taking turns to row in two-hour shifts.

Maurice realised, in that moment, that his captaincy was over. Any pretence that he was in charge had evaporated. All he could offer was doubt.

"How far do you think you can row in two hours?" he said. His tone must have given him away.

"We must try," said Maralyn.

As the sun dropped below the horizon, they ate their first dinner on the raft. One tin from their collection, which Maralyn heated up for three minutes in a small saucepan over the stove. The gas canister was half-used and they had no spares, but if Maralyn was careful about how much she used, it should last out the tins. They passed the saucepan back and forth between them, taking one spoonful at a time, in silence. For "afters," wrote Maralyn, they had a biscuit each.

When they finished, Maurice suggested that they wait a day to start rowing. In another twenty-four hours he thought they might reach the middle of the shipping lane, which passed south of the Galápagos. Maybe, just maybe, someone would come past. Maralyn agreed.

~

As they prepared for their first night on the raft, they noticed that its inflated tubes were already softening, making the base sag. Maurice found the emergency pump. *Pffft. Pffft.* Ludicrous, really, that all there was between them and the ocean was four and a half feet of thin material.

The air cooled. Darkness filled the sky. Stars followed, one by one, then in swaths, their light blinking on the moving water.

It was hardly what you'd call sleep. They couldn't extend their legs and had no covers, only oilskins, their clothes, and the canopy of the raft. Because they couldn't lie down at the same time, they took turns. Maralyn curled up in a ball while Maurice sat up and kept watch. Then they swapped. Maurice, being larger, took up most of the room whatever he was doing. They were so low down, it felt as if they were almost *in* the water, so close to the surface that they could feel every lap and swallow.

The breeze worked its way around their bodies. Something was alive in them, the kind of primal anxiety that prevents a mind from surrendering to sleep. On *Auralyn*, the ocean had been tempered by the hard wood of the hull and the rigid surface of a bunk. Now the water swelled beneath a layer of fabric, the kind of movement against which muscles, which long to forget themselves, start to brace. Unsupported, their bodies registered each rise and fall, the insecurity of every wave.

THREE

At dawn, they woke to an empty sky, an empty ocean. Nothing to see except themselves, already obsessed by thirst. They took turns sipping from their allotted pint. It was better, almost, to have nothing than to have a sip. Such a pathetic amount only seemed to reveal the depth of their need.

Maurice checked the containers in the dinghy and discovered that four gallons had been contaminated by seawater. They needed rain, but the sky was a hard blue. It seemed incapable of change, as if it could only ever be cloudless. They were used to moving fast through the water, air flowing past them. Now that they were still, the heat enclosed them like a tomb. From midday to four, they hid beneath the raft's canopy, dunked their spare clothes in the sea, and laid them on their bodies.

All day they looked for something, a ship, anything. But

they were the only anomaly, the single tree in the middle of a flat plain that attracts the lightning and burns.

~

The second night, under a high, clear moon, they began to row. Maurice wedged the compass between two water carriers to check they were going in the right direction. Once the moon had sunk, he used the stars: the polestar, low on the northern horizon, Orion, Crux, and the seven bright points of the Plough.

The problem was not so much the rowing itself, though it was tiring and painful, but having to tow the raft behind them. Every time Maurice pulled on the oars, the dinghy surged forwards and then stopped abruptly as the line between the dinghy and the raft tightened, robbing the dinghy of momentum. The raft then shifted in turn, catching up. The movement seemed token at best, a desultory heave. All that physical effort and they had barely moved. It was like trying to drag a tired child up a hill, their reluctance almost pulling you back down.

They rowed, two hours on, two hours off, for eight hours until the sun rose again. At one point, Maralyn thought she heard a plane overhead, the distinctive hum of engines, but when she looked, there was nothing there. Out at sea, as in the desert, things seemed to appear and disappear.

To keep them from dehydrating while they rowed, Maralyn doubled the water ration. It didn't help. Their thirst increasingly felt like an illness, a throb that infected every thought. They were racing through their supply. Maurice wasn't sure they'd be able to row far enough to reach the right latitude before they ran out of water. Maralyn refused to complain, or give in.

"I could not disillusion her," wrote Maurice, though he tried. Maralyn reminded him, instead, that it would soon be the wet season. The rains would come.

Maurice took a morning sight with the sextant, eager to know how far they had travelled after their night of rowing. It was impossible to get the measurement exactly right: The dinghy was always moving on the swell of the ocean, and they were so low in the water that his eyeline was only three feet above the sea. The horizon was therefore closer, making his calculations less accurate. He worked out, roughly, that they had rowed just over four miles south, and drifted nearly thirty miles west. Four miles! A pitiful distance.

Maralyn saw clouds in the distance. They must have gathered over the Galápagos, she thought. The islands couldn't be far away after all: A little more rowing and they'd get there. Maurice said nothing. What is there to say in the face of such delusion?

They rowed for three more nights. Blisters formed all over their hands. They realised, through exhaustion, that their strength was no longer endlessly renewable. The rowing might just take the rest of it.

At noon on 9 March, nearly a week since *Auralyn* had sunk, Maurice took another sight. Four nights of rowing and they had gained ten miles to the south. To reach the latitude of the

Galápagos, they would have to keep going for at least ten more nights, but the current was carrying them west faster than they could row. By that logic, they would never reach the islands, however hard they rowed.

The whole effort had been pointless. They should stop, Maurice suggested, save their bodies and their last pints of water, and hope for a ship.

Maralyn thought for a while. Then she climbed into the dinghy, picked up the oars, positioned them so they stood upright in the middle of the vessel, and tied a sail bag between them. If they couldn't row the dinghy, they could at least make it sail. Maurice couldn't help himself. "You'll be driving us northwest," he told her.

"And towards a shipping lane," Maralyn replied, "and the American coast!"

It was impossible to discourage her, even with facts. He knew that once they were out of the windless belt of the doldrums, they were likely to encounter the northeast trade winds, which would push them southwest, away from America. If they were lucky, they might meet a countercurrent running east. But Maralyn wasn't interested in probability. She was fixated on the shipping lane, the answer to their problems.

Maurice reminded her that the Pacific Ocean was not like the English Channel, teeming with ships. Remember Hiscock. They might go for weeks without seeing anything at all.

FOUR

After a string of blue days, the sky filled with fat clouds, stacked upwards like castles. The ocean became wild, waves frothing. "Motion violent," wrote Maralyn. Thunder clattered around them and lightning jagged across the sky. The storm was all noise, all light; more like a show than weather. It passed as quickly as it came, and without any rain.

That night, their first of no rowing, they had little rest. If they weren't being battered by wind, they were being hit by creatures, as if the storm had woken the ocean's inhabitants. Sharks circled and buffeted the raft. A turtle got caught in the dinghy ropes. They worried he might chew through them or take a bite out of the rubber. It took a long time to set him free.

Early on 12 March, Maralyn saw movement on the horizon. Even in the morning haze, when shapes suggest themselves and then dissolve, the hard, dark outline of a ship heading east was unmistakable.

A ship! Here it was, and only about a mile away. It hadn't taken so long, after all. They were saved.

She laid out the flares. Maurice shortened the line between the raft and the dinghy. As the ship drew level with them, Maralyn passed Maurice a smoke flare. He tore off the tape and tried to light it. Nothing.

"It's a dud. A bloody dud!" he shouted and threw it into the sea.

They tried another. Same again. Then a third. No light, no smoke. The flares were all they had to make themselves visible. Waving didn't work; they were too easily obscured by the swell. They needed blazing fireworks forty feet above them in the sky.

The ship kept sailing. The helplessness was horrifying. To be so close to people who had no idea you were there. Maurice could almost swim after it, if it would only slow down. He wanted to try another flare, but they had only three left, and the ship was now too far away to see them even if the next flare lit.

They watched it shrink back into the haze. Maurice gave up and sat back down in the dinghy. Maralyn kept waving her jacket. She knew it was pointless, but she couldn't just sit there knowing a ship was so close, even if all she could see was its funnel being sucked away into nothing.

They ate breakfast in silence. Maralyn wondered if it had been too early in the morning. Perhaps the crew had been eating below deck. They'd left the ship on autopilot and there was no one on deck to spot them. That must be it. A reasonable explanation. If someone had been up there, they'd have seen the raft in a second. Next time it would be different: The ship would pass later; someone would notice them.

It took such energy not to feel hopeless; such willpower. In truth, it was hard not to feel humiliated. All that waving. "We couldn't believe we were so hopeful for a little while," wrote Maralyn, as if she'd been tricked.

FIVE

At times, the Pacific appears like a wasteland. Scan the water and you'll see no movement, as if some terrible event has wiped the sea of its life. The ocean evolved from a super-ocean, the Panthalassic, which, 250 million years ago, covered almost three-quarters of Earth. It will not always be as it is, just as it is no longer what it once was.

In its deepest parts, the creatures living far beneath the surface have to make their own light. Squid trail lit tentacles, jellyfish flare like pinwheels, and the angler fish has a glowing bulb at the end of a rod that sticks up from its head, attracting prey into the black cave of its mouth. All this luminescent life is down there, busy with its work.

By chance, Maurice and Maralyn were adrift on a part of the ocean that was full of creatures. This close to the Galápagos, Darwin's "little world within itself," they were near a convergence of five ocean currents. The cold water from the Humboldt Current, travelling up from the Antarctic bearing penguins and seals, joins with two equatorial currents and the warmer Panama Current flowing down from Central America. The fifth current, the deep, cool Cromwell, wells up from three hundred feet below, carrying the disintegrating matter of decomposing organisms to the surface, which prompts the growth of plankton. Fish come to feed on the plankton. Birds are drawn to the fish. Where you have plankton, you have life.

Turtles often gathered around the raft, swimming in circles as if playing a game. Maurice and Maralyn enjoyed watching them at first, until the game seemed to change and they started ducking beneath the raft, bashing and rubbing themselves against its floor before popping out the other side. It felt as if they were being punched repeatedly in the bottom.

Maurice wondered if they were trying to dislodge parasites or barnacles from their heads, or find shelter from the sun. Or maybe they liked the feeling of scraping themselves against something, like a sheep with a post. Whatever it was, he started to worry that their hard shells would damage the thin underside of the raft. Some of the young ones had spines on their backs that might pierce the fabric. They started to bat them away with one of the raft paddles, but they kept coming back, undeterred.

What if they killed one and ate it, suggested Maralyn. Maurice wasn't sure. Neither of them *wanted* to kill a living creature, but their situation was bleak. Nearly two weeks adrift and they had run out of gas, their few remaining tins would have to be eaten cold, and their other supplies were low too. Killing a turtle was the practical solution: They needed more food, and turtles were both readily available and annoying. He had no counterargument.

When the next large one slammed itself against the raft, knocking the sextant case out of place, they grabbed a flipper each and hauled it out of the water onto the floor of the dinghy.

Maurice decided to knock it out first so the turtle wouldn't struggle or suffer too much. He raised one of the paddles into the air and smashed it down on the turtle's head. Then he held the turtle upside down over the seat of the dinghy and Maralyn tried to cut its head off. Their weapons were limited: a blunt mariner's knife, a penknife, some stainless steel scissors. Nothing seemed to work very well on its thick, sinewy neck. After several minutes of sawing, she'd barely left a mark.

The turtle woke and began to flap in panic. Maralyn was furious. She felt bad enough that they were killing the creature; it didn't need to make the task worse by reminding them it was alive. Maurice gripped the turtle tightly as it writhed so that Maralyn could keep hacking away. Eventually, she severed an artery and a stream of thick blood gushed over her hands. A bowl they'd placed beneath its neck was soon full. They'd heard of people drinking turtle blood, but they couldn't bring themselves to try it. Not yet. When they emptied the bowl into the sea, dark red swirling in the water, the fish flocked.

The dead turtle lay before them. Maralyn reasoned that cutting it up couldn't be that different from carving a chicken. Apart from its shell; that would have to go. Maurice worked his knife around the edge until they could prise the whole thing off. Underneath they discovered a layer of rich white meat.

Maralyn sliced four steaks out of each shoulder blade. The flavour wasn't terrible: delicate and savoury, not too tough. Some compare sea turtle to veal when it's cooked. They ate these raw.

Finished, they chucked the remains of the turtle's carcass over the side of the dinghy. As Maralyn washed her bloody hands in the water, fish swarmed towards her to suck at her fingers. It was obvious: They should fish.

Maurice went to fetch the fishhooks from the emergency bag. They weren't there. It seemed impossible. They *had* to be there. They had packed and repacked, checked and double-checked their supplies in Panama. Somehow, they must have left the hooks out. If ever there was an act of poor seamanship, surely this was it. What was the point of all those preparations if you left out something as vital as a fishhook?

Maralyn climbed back into the raft and found some safety pins and pliers. She bent the sharp point of a pin over to turn it into a hook, then tied on a cord with a single-loop Turle knot. Maurice watched her, doubtful that it would work. "We'll soon find out," she said.

She pierced a bit of turtle meat with the hook and dropped the line over the side of the raft into the water. The fish ravaged it, tearing it off the hook. She tried again and the same thing happened. Maurice noticed that some of the meat was wrapped in a membrane that might stop it from falling off the hook so easily. He passed Maralyn a chunk.

This time, the meat stayed where it was. Almost instantly, Maralyn yanked a silver fish out of the water. Maurice smacked it on the back of the head with the mariner's knife until it stopped moving. Maralyn kept fishing. Once they had enough for breakfast, Maurice gutted the fish, then separated out the liver and roe and sliced down the centre of each fish on its underside. Maralyn cut off their heads, then delicately cut the flesh away from the backbone. The eyes, which they gouged out, turned out to be full of liquid, which they drank. Anything close to water felt glorious. They divided up the meat between two bowls.

Maurice ate first, swallowing down the fat, wet lumps. Maralyn forced herself to eat a fillet before giving up, her throat closing in revulsion against the slippery flesh. She'd have to get over that, just as she would have to adjust to chewing raw turtle. There were many things to get over, after all, not least the indignity of going to the toilet in front of each other, crouched over an empty biscuit tin in the dinghy. They called it their "outside loo."

~

Killing soon became mechanical. It was like fishing in an overstuffed pond: Maurice could pluck them out of the water one after another.

They fished every morning and then again in the evening so the catch was fresh for dinner. Maralyn proposed a system: a bowl for the fillets and another for the skins; livers and roe in a mug and the eyes in a small tin. The skins were scraped of any meat, then thrown back into the water. They cut the fish heads in half and took out the sweet meat. They ate the gills occasionally, though that made them thirsty. Then they ate the livers, fillets, and eyes. A drink of water at the end. Their water supplies were now so low that they sucked moisture from the flesh of the fish.

The killings didn't always go smoothly. The next turtle they killed, a female, fought back, scratching their legs with her claws. Maurice couldn't keep her still. Her jaws snapped, and they worried she'd bite a hole out of the dinghy. Even upside down she could rotate herself by pushing her flippers against the sides of the dinghy. Maurice tried to grab her by the front flippers, but she pushed back. He felt his anger rise as Maralyn's had, indignant that the creature should bother to resist. To steady himself, he moved his feet closer to her body. The turtle bit his ankle. She wouldn't let go, jaws clamped around the bone. Maurice had to wrench his ankle out of her mouth, tearing off a layer of skin. He swore, then instructed Maralyn, "Get the knife and cut its throat."

Blood went everywhere. "How brutal life seemed as we examined our unfortunate victim," reflected Maurice. Afterwards, they rested in the dinghy and forced themselves to eat the blood once it had congealed. Then the normal dissection. Steaks, liver, kidneys, heart. No eggs but plenty of greenish fat, which they had almost grown to like and collected carefully. "I'll never eat turtle again after this escapade," wrote Maralyn in her diary.

~

Later, the turtles gave Maralyn an idea. Perhaps they could catch a larger one, attach it to the raft, and encourage it to pull them, like a horse in front of a cart, across the ocean.

A large male came close enough to catch. They held him

upside down in the water and hooked ropes over his rear flippers. As if he understood his mission, the turtle began to swim westwards, towards the Galápagos. He was so strong the water streamed back from his body in little waves, like a motorboat. They caught another one, and harnessed him too.

"I had visions of driving our 'team' right into harbour!" wrote Maralyn. A conqueror's vision, Romans in a chariot, coming over a hill and laying claim. A vision that was shattered almost immediately when the new turtle decided to swim fast in the opposite direction. The turtles, while alive, had minds of their own. They went back to killing them instead, apart from one, a small creature, who kept swimming up and down near the raft, as if it had something to tell them. They decided to keep it as a pet.

Every morning Maurice placed the turtle gently in the water with a rope tied round his rear flipper, and the creature swam while Maurice fished. After a while, when it grew too hot, they pulled him back in and covered him with wet rags. It helped, somehow, to have a living creature to look after beyond themselves.

SIX

There were ways of marking time, of trying to keep a grip on it. They had the sunrise and the sunset and the habits of their pet turtle, who would pull himself up onto the dinghy seat and watch them, wrote Maralyn, "with a sorrowful eye." Maralyn had her diary and began to write out a calendar on the canopy of the raft. Significant dates had a circle round them: Easter, Passover, birthdays. A cross when they caught a turtle, a plus sign for the sight of a ship.

Maurice had his watch, a Rotary Incabloc, which he hung from an electric wire on their broken emergency light. Sometimes Maralyn's hair caught on the winder, which stopped the watch. Maurice would have to wait for the sun to reach its zenith to reset the time.

At home, it would be nearly the beginning of spring, Maralyn realised. England would soon be coming into leaf. All that energy, turning into green. The country would be soaked by rain. “Sometimes I can smell the Eng countryside, fresh mown grass etc.,” she wrote in her diary. “I long for greenery and brown earth, plants and trees.”

When she woke early in the morning, in the gap between sleep and consciousness where fictions grow, she imagined she was camping in the Lake District. The orange of the raft’s canopy was the same colour as their tent. It wasn’t hard to believe, pressed against the warmth of Maurice’s body, that they were in their sleeping bags and that beyond the flaps of the tent were rising hills, sheep grazing, fields bordered by mossy stone walls. She could almost hear the birds.

Compared with land, the palette of the ocean was limited. A sunset could put on a show, striping the sky with fading colour, but mostly both water and sky shifted between greys and blues, or the black of night. The only colour they had on their vessels was a flag that Maurice had made from a pair of orange oilskin trousers, which he’d tied to an oar and attached to the seat in the dinghy: an attempt to make them visible.

~

On 14 March, as they were sheltering in the raft, they heard a rush of air, like something taking off. Maralyn poked her head out and there was a whale, twenty feet behind them.

Maurice felt strangely calm. There was nothing he could do, he knew. They were at its mercy. From the entrance of the raft, they watched it, though they were able to see only a portion of its body framed in the raft’s doorway, ribs visible through its shining black skin. It reminded Maralyn of a cow. The blowhole was almost close enough to touch. When it opened, slowly, a great cloud of droplets burst into the air and rained down on them in the raft.

Maurice took Maralyn's hand. If the whale struck the raft and they capsized, he whispered, he might struggle to rescue her. Hold on to the ropes. Maralyn nodded.

They sat there, silent, the whale peaceful and still. What was it doing? Monitoring their movements, or keeping them company perhaps. It wasn't really their question to ask. They were the ones trespassing. After what felt like hours but was only minutes, they saw its bulk surge forward and down.

"Don't dive now," whispered Maralyn, worried that a sudden movement would capsize them. The whale dived, but cleanly, the black flukes of its tail suddenly high and dark against the sky, then sliding below the surface without a splash.

They stared at the place where it had been. No trace. No blood. "What a pity we didn't take a photograph," said Maralyn. "No one will believe us when we talk about it."

Maurice was amazed. How much she seemed to assume: that they'd be rescued, that they'd live to turn an encounter with a whale into an anecdote, as if this ordeal were a minor interruption to the progress of their lives. No part of Maralyn appeared to question their survival.

~

After the whale, the weather changed. Still no rain, but the days grew cooler, the wind stronger. The waves started to build. As the wind whipped up the ocean, spray found its way into the raft where the canopy joined the inflated tubes. Maurice and Maralyn mopped continuously, squeezing out sponges over the side. To brace themselves against the surging waves, they lowered the raft's insubstantial sea anchor into the water. It lasted only a day before coming loose. Maurice replaced it with a pair of oilskin trousers that steadied them enough to allow them to fish. Meanwhile, the raft kept swinging in front of the dinghy, which made the linking rope entangle with a bottle of carbon dioxide attached to the raft's bottom, used to reinflate it. Every time the line got caught on the bottle it made the raft spin. In the raft's open doorway, the waves came fast towards them. Facefuls of ocean. All the spray falling into the raft made the base constantly wet. They sat in pools of water like plant pots in saucers, their skin rubbing against the floor. Sores quickly developed on their legs and bottoms.

At last, on 24 March, the clouds gathered and the rains came. They had waited so long it had come to seem almost impossible that fresh, drinkable water could fall freely from the sky. Any pain was forgotten as they worked out how to collect it. A steady drip, they noticed, fell from the raft's ventilation duct and lookout window. They placed a bucket underneath it and after about an hour had collected a pint. The water was yellow and tasted awful and rubbery, presumably from the canopy's waterproof coating. They chucked it over the side and tried again. Another hour; drip, drip, drip. This batch tasted marginally better, or they decided not to mind so much. They scooped the water out of the bucket with a mug and transferred it into a plastic container to store in the dinghy.

Two hours of rain for one pint of rubbery water wasn't a very reassuring equation, but at least they had a fresh supply that could be topped up every time it rained. And at least it wasn't salt water, which was everywhere and useless.

After two days of storms, they had managed to replace all their original water. Endless collecting and mopping had exhausted them. On the night of the twenty-sixth, the sky finally cleared. Maurice, on first watch, saw meteorites sparking into nothing and was briefly disoriented, still unused to the constellations at this latitude. Gradually the patterns clarified and he saw the Dog Star, Sirius, the brightest in the sky; Rigel, in the corner of Orion; and Capella, the little goat.

There weren't many ways of being alone out on the ocean. They were profoundly alone, but they were still *they*, yoked together, like the dinghy and the raft. During the night, on watch, it was different, as if he were the only person alive in the universe. He shined his torch at his watch. He'd let her sleep a little longer.

Maurice's thoughts turned towards himself. Why he was the way he was. If only he could be different. How much he wanted to be different. A lifetime, really, of thinking like this.

"From my meditations came clear resolutions for the future," he wrote. "Resolutions that would affect my entire attitude to people." A grand plan, then. Their time adrift would not be for nothing. Maurice would transform.

From now on, he told himself, he would listen to people's arguments with patience and compassion. It was difficult to tolerate other people when they were obviously wrong, but he would change. And he would change his behaviour in his marriage, too. "I resolved to improve my selfish approach to our endeavours," he wrote, "and to reduce my ego to equable proportions." The things we see when we look at a night sky; the things we think. Usually, the stars lend perspective, a leavening sense of one's own insignificance. Maurice looked up and saw only himself, only his flaws; the hope that he might become someone better.

SEVEN

Three weeks adrift, and Maurice's skeleton seemed to be trying to find a way out of his body. Maralyn could count his ribs. Their faces were beginning to ache where their skulls were pushing through taut skin.

Towards the end of March, they ate the last piece of Dundee cake for breakfast. They would have to go down to half rations, Maralyn decided. The fish and turtles didn't seem to fill them up. A diet of raw protein and rainwater wasn't enough. They needed potatoes. Wheat. Heft.

Maralyn asked Maurice how she looked. Maurice seemed reluctant to reply. He had always found her beautiful, and she'd seemed more attractive than ever in the Caribbean and Panama: tanned and slim, with a physical confidence and agility on the boat that seemed to ripple through her body.

Now he saw the flesh fall from her face day by day, lines

carving around her mouth and eyes, as though she were ageing at speed. Her shoulder blades stuck out of her back. He found he had no hunger for her at all; not cruelly, but as if even the possibility of arousal had been switched off. He felt he'd become asexual, as though his body were too preoccupied by the business of staying alive to entertain the idea of anything else. They were squatting over a tin in the dinghy every day. It was hardly the setting for desire.

Maralyn's interest was more pragmatic than aesthetic in any case. She hadn't had a period since their boat sank. Anything can do it: stress, exhaustion, a sudden loss of weight. Her body was shutting down. She wanted to know how bad things were and she needed Maurice to tell her. For good or ill, sometimes we can see ourselves only through the eyes of a partner, as though they have greater access to reality, or at least a version undistorted by our own thoughts.

Eventually, Maurice admitted that her face looked gaunt. There wasn't much point in lying. She could see her own legs, couldn't she? Bruised and thin, kneecaps pushing through the skin. She could feel her lips cracking from thirst, like his.

They tried their best. Their few remaining clothes were hardly wearable, either rotting or saturated in salt that rubbed painfully against their skin, but they still had oilskins for when it rained, and shirts to protect them from the sun. They attempted to wash, but their soap was disintegrating and didn't lather in the salt water. "We threw it into the sea in disgust," wrote Maralyn, as if this once useful object had betrayed them.

They still had a comb at least. Maurice's hair was easy to look after. There wasn't much of it, though his beard was growing fast. When his moustache started finding its way into his mouth, Maralyn trimmed it.

If only her own hair were so straightforward. Every morning, she spent fifteen minutes trying to untangle the knots. "How often I threatened to cut it off, but resisted!" It would be too symbolic. No one cuts off all their hair without it meaning *something*. A protest, a refutation; a nun-like shunning of the world. She wasn't quite there yet.

EIGHT

In the black dark before dawn on 29 March, a red light appeared above the waves in the distance. Maralyn was on watch. She stared at the light, unwilling to trust it. Then she saw more lights, probably from a masthead.

Maralyn shook Maurice awake. They found their last two flares. They could see a tanker coming towards them, glowing with light from its deck and through its portholes from cabins, where people must be sleeping or just waking, thinking, talking. Warm bodies, being alive.

Maurice tried to light the first flare. It didn't take. He hurled it into the sea without a word. He tried the second and briefly, the water, raft, and dinghy were all pooled in bright white. How could they not be seen? They were the only thing to see.

The flare faded, their last one. The ship carried on. Maurice flashed his torch. SOS. As if a torch, after that blaze of firework, could do anything at all.

"The 2nd ship in 25 days," wrote Maralyn in her diary. "Maybe it will be 3rd time lucky."

They watched the ship sail on until its stern light shrank to a dot and became just another point of light in the sky, indistinguishable from the rest.

~

The third ship came nearly two weeks later, on 10 April. Maurice was fishing, and therefore unreachable. It was as if he were back at the printing press. Locked into a technical task, he could shut out the world. Maralyn had to shout. "Can't you see the ship?!"

He looked up and saw nothing but ocean. "Behind you!"

He turned. There it was, a freighter sailing east, towards Panama.

"I could hear it from inside the raft," she said, wondering at his incapacity.

They had no more flares, so they waved their oilskins. It was as if they were waving at the moon. The ship ploughed on, motoring past with such disregard that it made them question their very existence.

"Were we invisible?" wrote Maralyn. "We were both very depressed and couldn't understand why no one had seen us." They were in a shipping lane with vessels going past. They should, by rights, be seen. "Surely," she wrote, "it was time for a change of fortune?"

Bad luck confirmed Maurice's worldview, but it played havoc with Maralyn's. She believed in almost everything, bar God. She believed in luck and fortune, in third time lucky. "Destiny, fate, kismet, call it what you will," she wrote. "I believe that each happening in our lives prepares us for some eventual test." All this hardship had meaning; it laid out a path.

But being passive in the face of such forces didn't suit her either. They could make their own luck. "If we want something badly enough," she wrote, "through sheer determination often that goal is achieved. I didn't want to die and I was doing everything in my power to make sure I lived."

In Maralyn's view, either they were meant to survive or they would engineer their own survival, a two-pronged approach that left no room for failure. After all, she needed every available argument to defend herself against Maurice's gloom. In a situation in which believing in the possibility of survival, however unlikely, was the key to survival itself, Maurice's pessimism was like a weight dragging them down. To keep him alive, she had to keep his hope alive, and to do that, she needed not only her own stubborn faith but something larger than herself. A cosmic theory, as backup.

But Maurice couldn't follow her. "Her faith in some supernatural power governing our affairs never weakened," he wrote. To Maurice, it was pure fiction. Like all fictions, her story gave shape to chaos. He could see why she liked it, why it was seductive, but it bore no relation to reality.

Their situation was a result of his failure, certainly not the master plan of some higher force. There was no more meaning in the number of ships, or the sinking of *Auralyn*, than in the accident of his birth. There were two possible outcomes: They would live or they would die. The result would be decided by the rough unfolding of events. A ship might see them, or it might not. They might be drowned in a storm, or they might not. They might die of starvation or disease, or they might not. They could *try* to survive, but otherwise things would happen as they happened.

Unless they killed themselves first, which was the only definitive choice they—or anyone else for that matter—could make about their lives.

~

When the fourth ship came, two days after the third, Maralyn heard it first. Those ears.

She froze, then crawled to the opening of the raft. It was the afternoon and the sun was low in the sky, the waves rising in the southeasterly wind. She couldn't see anything, but the sound was clear now. Maurice eventually heard the mechanical thrum of distant engines. There it was: a white ship sailing south, about half a mile away, flashing in and out of view among the waves. Maurice climbed into the dinghy and fetched the Dundee cake tin. Maralyn's new idea was to make their own smoke flares by burning damp paper in the tin and kerosene-dipped rags wrapped around coat hangers. Maurice poured methylated spirits onto the paper in the tin, placed the tin in an empty turtle shell, lit the paper with a match, and then held the shell above his head. There wasn't enough smoke. He put it back on the floor of the dinghy, grabbed a wet towel, dampened down the flames, and clouds of smoke billowed into the air. The wind blew the smoke sideways, but at least it was visible.

Maralyn waved her oilskin from the raft. "It's stopping," she shouted. "Now it's turning!"

It was. It was turning towards them. Someone must have seen them. The ship turned a full semicircle until it seemed to be facing them.

Then it seemed to pause, as if thinking. Maralyn kept waving, and Maurice started to wave too, his tin nearly out of smoke. To have turned, someone must have spotted them, a person on the bridge. Perhaps they noticed the smoke, or a flap of oilskin, a flash of orange as a wave lifted the raft above the swell.

So why wasn't it coming towards them? Why turn and not come towards them?

The ship moved. It was hard to see which way it was going. The distance distorted things. But it seemed to be turning, it *was* turning, another semicircle, away from them. Then it stopped again, bobbing up and down in the water. The pause, containing hope, was worse.

Maurice waved until his arm ached. "Come on," he yelled. "Don't keep us waiting!"

The ship began to sail away from them, back on course. Its outline softened and the bulk of it shrank until it was a small blot on the sky, then nothing. Once it was gone, it was hard to believe it had ever been there at all.

Maurice looked at Maralyn. It was as if hope had left her body. He'd never seen her look so crushed.

"How could they not have seen us?" she said, in disbelief.

He tried to comfort her. The sun was low. The ship's crew had probably been blinded by the glare. Perhaps they had seen them and then lost them again, squinting in the brightness. Maybe someone else had taken a quick look, seen nothing, and dismissed the idea.

"Always our luck so bad!" Maralyn wrote later in her diary. But it wasn't enough that they were just unlucky. There was a reason they'd survived this long, she told Maurice. They were *meant* to survive. There was a reason the ship hadn't come back for them: It wasn't the ship that was *meant* to rescue them. No, the ship that would rescue them, she told Maurice with confidence, the pieces locking into place, would be a large black Russian container ship, sailing east towards Panama.

~

Less than a week later it came, the ship that was meant to rescue them. There were some deviations from her vision. It was sailing west, not east, and it seemed doubtful that it was a Russian container ship, but who could say for sure in the middle of the night. All they could make out were the portholes in the darkness, glowing like a row of low moons in the distance.

Maurice pulled the dinghy close to the raft and clambered in. Maralyn passed him one of their homemade coat-hanger flares. He dipped it into the kerosene; she poured over the methylated spirits and lit a match. It wouldn't take. The wind was too strong, and even when she cupped her hands around the shivering flame of the match, the rags didn't catch. She told Maurice to try the torch. The batteries had almost run out, and all it emitted was a thin, faltering beam. The ship sailed on, lights fading into the dark.

They went back to their places in the raft without a word.

Maralyn felt something turn in her. The ships were disturbing their peace: If they weren't going to stop, she didn't want to see them either. If there'd been curtains on the raft—curtains she'd have doubtless sewn herself—she would have drawn them now.

~

In the morning, they examined the kerosene container and found it almost full of water. They emptied it and gave up on the idea of using flares again. A few days later, they discovered that even their matches had become damp.

It was hardly surprising, given that everything in the raft was constantly wet. But to Maralyn, the sodden matches were a sign. They weren't giving up on their plans and objects; their plans and objects were giving up on *them.* They weren't ignoring the ships; the ships were ignoring *them.* It was a conspiracy of sorts: the flares, the matches, the ships, all working in concert to defeat them.

Later, she spread the remaining matches out in the sun to dry them. When she tried to light them, their heads fell off.

NINE

In April, the rains came in earnest. Helpful for replenishing their water stocks; awful for morale. "Weather miserable—like us," wrote Maralyn in her diary. "Depressed."

Six weeks after *Auralyn* had sunk, six weeks of subsisting on the raft, wet, under-slept, and underfed, they were both worn out and had diarrhoea. They wondered if some of their water supplies had been contaminated by turtle excrement.

At dawn on 20 April, Maurice climbed across to the dinghy and discovered that their turtle was dead. They were struck by sadness. They'd loved him, in a way. He'd been their pet, become part of the family. A brief pause, then they ate him.

The weather became relentless. The wind roared and they were hurled around like flotsam on the swell. They were used to storms after months at sea, but it was different in a raft that spun and lurched, as insubstantial and weightless as a bath toy.

All they could do was grip the ropes on the side as it rose and fell, and wait for the weather to pass. Even if another ship came, they knew they couldn't be seen when the waves were so high. The ocean, usually an expanse, walled them in.

At night, they struggled to keep watch. Their heads nodded on to their chests. Maurice stayed awake while Maralyn tried to sleep with her head resting against the top tube of the raft. At midnight, they swapped and Maurice curled up on the floor like a foetus.

The effort felt token, but they refused to abandon watch entirely. That felt too close to giving up. Keeping watch is the most important duty on board a ship, and somehow the most symbolic. Every member of a crew takes their turn, each carrying the mantle of responsibility until it is passed to the next person. For those hours, you are the boat's sole protector. Abandon post, and you might as well abandon ship.

TEN

Doubt grows in emptiness.

Some years ago, a pilot in California crashed his small plane over the mountains of the High Sierra. He left behind his two passengers and hiked alone for nine days over mountains and through forests, eating snow, until he came to a road and found help. The trek had been arduous; the pilot arrived in a café hurt and bedraggled and hungry. But the journey had given him purpose and something to do. When the pilot returned to the plane, he found his passengers dead, one trapped in the wreckage, the other a little distance away. Able only to sit and wait, what could they do but die?

It is not so much the feats of endurance that keep people alive as the absence of surrender. Maurice, lacking occupation, became desolate. There was no evidence to convince him that survival was likely, and he found it hard to believe in things he couldn't see. What was the point of trying?

Maralyn tried to distract him. They took turns reading aloud from their two books, discussing every word, every line. They told each other the plots of books they'd read in the past, or stories they remembered, like the one about an American soldier captured during the Korean War. To stay sane in solitary confinement, he designed and built a house in his mind. Maralyn found herself thinking of the medieval Queen Eleanor of Aquitaine, imprisoned for fifteen years by her husband Henry II after she'd colluded in a plot against him. Cut off from the world in the royal castle of Old Sarum in Wiltshire, a high-walled fortress on a hill surrounded by deep ditches, wasn't so different, perhaps, from being adrift on a raft at sea.

They played games. All Maralyn's doing. She made a cat's cradle with a spare piece of string. They took turns to pick a word and then listed as many four-letter words as they could find within it. Dominoes were made from strips of paper torn out of the logbook. They soon realised that they couldn't play properly because the pieces of paper would simply blow away or get wet when they laid them down end to end. Instead, having dealt out their dominoes, they held them in their hands and wrote down each move on a piece of paper that they passed back and forth.

Playing cards would work better, Maralyn thought. It took half a day to make them, drawing on the hearts, diamonds, spades, and clubs with a pencil. The paper was so thin it was possible to see the other person's hand, so they had to be strict about not looking. They played whist, game after game, although they could play only on dry days because the cards fell apart in water. Maurice suggested he could teach Maralyn bridge, but decided it was too complicated. They wished they had chess.

Keeping Maurice busy wasn't enough, Maralyn realised. She had to give him something to believe in. On a blank ocean, she had little to work with, apart from what she could imagine. She began to talk "of our life before and during the voyage and what it would be like afterwards."

Afterwards! It was almost impossible for Maurice to think of such a time, as if this were how they'd always lived and how they always would. He tried to go along with it, but the best he could come up with was the opposite of their current state. England, solid ground, a house with a garden. Weather mitigated by walls and windows. Vegetables and flowers that they would tend through the seasons. A safe life, rakes in hand, feet lodged in the soil.

Maralyn suspected this was for her sake. "He was now prepared to give up this life, swallow the anchor and return to the life he had found so restricting, because he was convinced I would no longer wish to sail."

In fact, in the dead hours on the raft, leaning over the side, watching the fish circling and darting below, she'd been conjuring their next boat, just as the soldier in Korea had imagined his house. "A sleek white two-masted sailing boat. A thing of beauty, yet purposeful." She'd imagined it so fully she could wander round the vessel in her mind, see its furnishings and varnished woodwork, the scheme of the galley and the storage for the crockery. Everything was arranged just how she wanted. A house might have been a comfort initially, but it wouldn't last.

"Deep down within us both was the restless urge to travel," she wrote. "We had to go on."

Maurice didn't believe her. As if, after all this, she would want to go back to sea. She'd been dreaming of green, hadn't she? The comfort of grass.

Maralyn had to persuade him. This was their chosen existence, not a hobby or an experiment. It was more a manifesto than a lifestyle. You don't walk away from a choice like that after one mishap; it would be like abandoning a faith because you weren't blessed with a miracle.

In her version of the future, they would go back to England, build another boat, and live on it just as they had with *Auralyn*. Once it was ready, they'd embark on their next adventure.

~

Well, then. A project. Maralyn sketched a rough layout of the new boat in her diary. Maurice calculated its exact specifications. They amended the plans until they were happy; then Maurice attempted the first designs. External drawings and internal drawings. Drawings of the galley and drawings of the rigging. Aerial-view drawings and annotated drawings.

Maralyn made a list of the necessary provisions. They discussed how much food, exactly, they would need for a long voyage and how they'd stow it, endlessly reconfiguring the locker space to make it work. Maralyn plotted menus, writing down not only what she would cook but how and in what order. She talked Maurice through the dishes step by step, noting every ingredient. They agreed on the menu for their first meal on their new boat: iced melon, roast pork, applesauce, potatoes, cauliflower and cheese sauce, chocolate pudding, cheese and biscuits, chocolate mints. A four-course feast. They talked so much about the meals they might eat that they started to argue about them. Maurice thought they should have wine with curry; Maralyn disagreed. You had to have water with curry, she said, because the wine lost its taste with the spice.

Maralyn's diary started to fill up with menus for dinner parties, lunch parties, tea parties, for every meal of the day and alternatives at every meal, not just cereal and toast at breakfast, for example, but every kind of cereal and eggs cooked any way you liked.

> *B/fasts: Weetabix—hot & cold, Cornflakes, Porridge, Farley's Rusks, Varieties, Shredded Wheat, Rice Krispies, Sugar Smacks*
>
> *Fruit:—Grapefruit, melon, prunes*
>
> *Cooked:—sausages, bacon, egg, beans, tomatoes, boiled egg, scrambled egg, kippers, poached egg on toast*
>
> *Bread:—Bread & butter or toast & marmalade. (Croissants) or Scotch pancakes.*
>
> *DRINK: Tea or coffee*

For her dinner parties, she imagined multiple courses, each stuffed with various vegetables, feasts of pineapples and gammon, potatoes mashed *and* roasted, more potato, you'd think, than anyone was capable of consuming. The puddings were hefty: sponges and treacles and creams, and always, to round things off, coffee and mints or biscuits. They were like musical compositions, these menus, structured into movements.

> *1) 6 people. 4 botts wine 2 white 2 red Starter:—G/fruit & mandarin cocktail*
>
> *Main:—Gammon steak, sausage, pineapple, roasties, peas & sweetcorn. Tubs of potato and coleslaw salad, mushrooms*
>
> *Sweet:—Cherry flan, apple pie & fresh cream*
>
> *A/W:—Cheese, cream crackers or selection of cheeses Coffee & box liqueurs*
>
> *Or if it's cold—soup & hot rolls*
>
> *Lamb chops, sausage, onion sauce, roasties, mash and gravy*
>
> *Sponge pud, treacle & custard Cheese, biscs + coffee*
>
> *2) 4 people 2 botts wine*
>
> *Starter:—Pate, toast & salad*
>
> *Main:—Pork chops in breadcrumbs, sausage, A/sauce, roasties and mash, peas and carrots*
>
> *Sweet:—Apple & plum pie + ice cream Coffee & mints*
>
> *OR starter—Melon*
>
> *Main:—Veal, Yorks, roasties, mash, cauliflower + cheese sauce, mushrooms, roast onions*
>
> *Sweet:—Steamed choc pud + choc sauce*
>
> *After:—Cheese & biscs*
>
> *Coffee & mints*

Formal entertaining (6)

1. *Mandarin & grapefruit topped with cherry*
2. *Grilled trout*
3. *Roast leg of lamb, roasties, turnip mash, onion sauce, apple sauce, peas, beans, carrots*
4. *Frozen cream cake, ice cream & wafer*
5. *Cheese and biscuits*
6. *Coffee & mints*

Sometimes, she wrote lists of the options within a specific category of food, as if to remind herself of the possibilities.

Cakes

Swiss rolls Choc cake Madeira cake Ginger cake

Walnut cake Angel cake Dundee cake Fruit cakes Oaties Battenburg Egg custard Viennese whirls Chelsea cakes

The cakes, in particular, took on a kind of life of their own.

Cakes to bake for Maurice

Lemon cake lemon butter icing inside & sides, plain iced top, covered in crystallised fruit

Lemon cake covered in orange and buttercream, side topped with mandarins

Madeira cake with walnuts in cake, sandwiched by vanilla buttercream covered in marzipan & iced top and covered with walnuts

Coconut loaf

Banana loaf

A Mars special choc sponge sandwich with choc butter icing and layer of Mars bars, top with choc buttons and buttercream sides with squares of Mars bar pushed in

Swiss Roll

Perhaps it was the abundance of cake making that made it so pleasurable to think about: the quantity of sugar, a hunk of yellow butter, fresh eggs cracking on the side of a bowl, clouds of flour. A cake is so simple in its effect: comfort dressed up in coloured sugar, served on a special plate at teatime, the most pointless and English of meals. Not really a meal at all, but a display, for guests and birthday parties, for afternoon concerts and village fetes.

Sunday Tea (8–10 ple)

1 plate of meat paste sandwiches

1 plate of salmon and cucumber sandwiches

1 plate of cheese & beetroot

1 plate of cream cheese

1 plate of egg & tomato sandwiches

1 plate of bread & jam

1 plate of scones buttered

1 plate of doughnut rings

1 plate of tarts—mixed

1 plate of choc & madeira cake Jelly & fruit & cream

It was the food of childhood: little sandwiches and tablecloths. Everyone in their best dresses, crumbs down the front. The scones would be buttered, the tarts mixed, the sandwiches would be in brown *and* white bread.

When you're dying of starvation, all you can think about is food.

ELEVEN

By the time Maralyn's birthday came around, on 24 April, they had been adrift for seven weeks. Before they'd set off, she'd made a plan to meet friends on the Marquesas Islands in the South Pacific and share the Dundee cake, now long gone. The Marquesas were three thousand miles from the nearest continental landmass. European colonisers to the islands had thrust Catholicism and small white-painted churches on their people, in the brutish assumption that such things would improve them. Maralyn had wanted to bring only a cake.

Maurice decided to catch one of the silvery fish, their favourite, for a celebratory meal. It took some time; the fish kept nibbling at the bait but not biting. Finally, he got one. Huge and heavy, it made the line taut. Maralyn could see it trying to wrench itself off. Just as Maurice tried to yank the creature into the dinghy, it pulled free, catapulting the hook back into the rubber of the dinghy. As Maurice pulled it out, they heard the high, lethal hiss of air. Bubbles formed on the surface of the ocean where air was leaking into the water.

The puncture was just beneath the waterline. Maralyn quickly took all the water containers out of the dinghy and shoved them into the raft. They climbed in too, so that Maralyn could lift the dinghy out of the water while Maurice cleaned and dried the hole, then squeezed on a layer of glue. Her arms started to ache from holding the vessel up, so Maurice took her place and she applied a second coat of glue and a small black patch over the hole. They kept the dinghy out of the water until they were sure the glue was dry, then examined the patch. They hadn't done a bad job, especially considering that carrying the dinghy had been a torture for their wasted arms.

Once the dinghy was back in the water, they started transferring the water containers back. Maurice thought one was missing.

"Are you sure you've counted properly?" asked Maralyn.

"Well, you count and see if I'm right."

Maralyn counted. She counted again. He was right; there *was* one missing. Four gallons of water, gone. Enough to last four days. An amount of water that could, in a dry spell, keep them alive. Water floating away on water.

"To try and raise our spirits," wrote Maralyn, "I reminded Maurice that today *was* my birthday, and tonight we would celebrate."

They had one remaining tin of rice pudding. Maralyn opened it and they ate it topped with treacle in a kind of religious silence. The taste, creamy, rich, and sweet, filled them with pleasure, the way a drug streams around the nervous system. Something was off. They looked at the empty tin and saw that the metal within was red and flaking; the rice pudding had been tainted with rust.

~

The problems, after that, came in droves. A few days later, they noticed that the black patch on the dinghy was missing. They checked again. It was like the water bottle; they couldn't quite trust what they saw, or didn't see.

The patch had gone. Some of the glue had lodged in the hole, which slowed the escaping air, but the dinghy was now constantly deflating. They had to pump it up at least twice a day to keep it functional.

Then, on 28 April, they woke to find themselves sunk in a hollow in the middle of the raft. The bottom tube had deflated. On inspection, Maurice found a row of small holes. Maralyn blamed the spinefoot fish. They'd seen them gathering round the raft, often retreating to the shade beneath the vessel. Whenever a predator neared, their spines shot up, and this prickly defence must have punctured the bottom of the raft.

It hardly seemed possible that they now had holes in both vessels. The ocean had become a subtle enemy, unhooking water bottles, prising off a patch, rusting tins, dribbling into their craft, and making their bodies sore, as if it were engaged in some kind of guerrilla warfare, finding any way it could to creep into their territory and destroy it, without them even knowing until it was too late. It's only what water does to land, after all:

a quiet invasion over time, gradually eroding coastlines until houses fall into the sea and villages disappear from the map.

They dug out the instruction pamphlet for fixing the raft. It was laughable. They were supposed to dry the damaged area, rub it with emery paper, apply a coat of glue, allow it to dry, apply another coat of glue, wait until it was *almost* dry and then apply the patch.

They took an hour over the job, unable to hold the raft still as the waves pitched beneath them. As soon as they put it back in the water, the patch drifted away. It had barely lasted a minute.

The raft, without a strong lower tube, would be unstable and even more vulnerable than before. One more hole and the whole thing would surrender.

Maralyn opened the last tin of condensed milk. The shot of sugar gave them enough energy to discuss what to do. But what choice did they have? They couldn't forsake the raft: It was their only shelter. Without it they would be dangerously exposed to the sun and rain. They'd have to cope with it as it was, fatally weakened, like them.

Trying to sleep in a half-deflated raft was a new kind of agony. The base was now almost always soft beneath them, and the material pinched at their flesh. Their weight made the floor sag and pitch inwards so they fell into the middle. To maintain any passable impression of solidity, they had to pump two or three times an hour. If they gave up out of exhaustion, they would wake to find their bodies trapped in the bunched material. "Pumping every 20 mins all thro night," Maralyn wrote in her diary. "Despair & depression—no hope."

Reality remade itself yet again. Problems, it seemed, moved up and down a hierarchy. Things like finding food or gathering drinking water, which had once seemed impossible, now seemed minor, and had been replaced by other things, like a collapsing life raft, which were insurmountable.

The only relief came in the few moments after the raft was repumped and before the sinking began again. Brief seconds of solidity, when they were held above the ocean; a kind of heightened suspension, because they knew it wouldn't last.

Now and then, in brighter moments, Maurice liked to entertain the idea that they had become at one with the Pacific, able to cohabit with its creatures as if they were of the water themselves. But times like this exposed the absurdity of such a view. Living on an ocean was possible only with a range of functioning, man-made defences to mitigate the experience. They could survive when separated from the water by a solid hull, which even then needed regular attention to remain effective. Boats, like humans, are in a state of permanent decline. Every time a boat touches the water, it degrades. It was so obvious. They were not meant to be here.

"If we need help now is the time," wrote Maralyn on 29 April. "2 months living like this is beginning to play havoc with us." She had no energy left to pretend. "Despair is v. near the surface and death stares us in the face—if only a ship would rescue us—but we have very little hope for such a miracle."

~

After that, Maralyn didn't have much room left to write in her diary. She'd already filled up the rest of the pages with menus, lists, and drawings, covering May and June with doodles of cats and the occasional dress design.

Elbow length. Brown velvet. Slightly gathered panels cut full. Brown and pink paisley. If ok make green one—straight long sleeves and edge sleeves and collar with crochet (bought) cuffs.

And a skirt.

Panelled tailored camel coloured long skirt. Wear with brown or green blouse, pref brown.

To keep writing, Maralyn found paper wherever she could, tearing it out of the back of the logbook. Maurice noticed that she often seemed to be bent over a page, pencil rushing across. The silence of the work was excluding, like a secret between her and the words.

Mostly, Maralyn wrote letters to June. She was never going to send them, even if they survived. Just writing them was enough, the closest she could come to talking to someone else; someone who wasn't Maurice. Writing out the horror and the fear. Writing all the things she couldn't say to Maurice, because they were *about* Maurice. She knew that if he ever saw what she'd written, he'd be hurt.

It is possible to write yourself out of loneliness. Possible, too, to write yourself into being. As her body shrank, Maralyn built herself out of words, sentence by sentence. When she noted the happenings of the day, however bleak, the day was proven to be real and her faculties intact. The writing was the proof. The lists, the menus, and the clothes were reminders that such things still existed. Solid things, on solid ground, that she could make with her own hands. She was still alive. Look, it said so on the page.

If any of her papers got wet, she would spend hours drying them in the sun, handling them with the kind of care usually reserved for ancient texts, or as if they contained some vital formula whose loss would be incalculable.

TWELVE

April turned to May. "Yesterday both of us were v. depressed and reckoned the end wasn't far away," wrote Maralyn.

The canopy's waterproof coating had now worn away. When it rained, the inside of the raft became drenched. Waves regularly poured over the sides because the punctured tube meant they were sitting even lower in the ocean. The sun had turned the drinking water in one of their containers green. They tried to drink it anyway and were soon doubled over in pain, stomachs in revolt. They checked the other containers: all green. They had only two one-gallon containers left in the raft. Everything seemed to be on the turn. A milkfish they'd saved specially for their evening meal went bad, and made Maralyn vomit all night.

Maralyn, as low as she'd ever been, searched for something to hold on to. They had survived sixty days and the round number, she felt, must have meaning. She noted how rare it was for a couple to have such a period of uninterrupted time together. They had no secrets from each other, and a total absence of self-consciousness. You could, if you chose, see their way of existing as a privilege.

They argued, inevitably. How could they not? They'd say hurtful things and Maralyn would cry. Quickly enough, the argument would pass and they'd unpick it, see why they had snapped or become intolerant, and apologise. Even in the arguments, she could find light, sensing that they were developing a deeper respect for each other's opinions.

On 5 May, storms rolled in and the rain fell. As quickly as they could, they replaced all the stagnant water with fresh. Though it was impossible to fish in the surging sea, they caught another turtle, which they killed and tied to the back of the raft as a makeshift sea anchor. It was enough to lift Maralyn's mood: As long as they had drinkable water and something to eat, even the most violent squalls were tolerable.

The next morning, Maurice, hungry, ate some of the old turtle bait they'd kept. Maralyn told him to stop, but it was too late. He was soon hunched over the tin, and had diarrhoea for days.

~

Two days later, on 8 May, the sixth ship, a cargo vessel heading east, passed them. It happened to be Maralyn's mother's birthday. She could have sent Ada a telegram, telling her the good news of their rescue. That would have been a nice way to celebrate. The ship didn't pause.

The next ship would save them, said Maralyn. The lucky seventh. She calculated, based on current rations and the state of their health, that they could survive for another two weeks. Enough time, surely, for the seventh ship to arrive.

For the next ten days it rained without stopping. Maralyn couldn't remember the last time the raft had been dry. Maurice began to cough from somewhere deep in his lungs. There was a rattle in his breathing. He knew these sensations well, or at least his body did, the memory embedded in its cells. Months alone in a room.

On 18 May, at last, the sun came back. Just before midday, Maurice glanced out of the raft and saw a huge white cargo ship with a blue hull coming towards them. The lucky seventh.

They assumed their positions: Maurice in the dinghy, Maralyn in the raft. Maralyn passed Maurice the oilskins. They waved and shouted until their arms were sore and their voices hoarse. The ship sailed on.

THIRTEEN

So, they wouldn't be rescued. That seemed clear enough. They'd had their chances. Logically, then, death was imminent. They were already visibly dying, their muscles atrophying, organs straining, eye sockets sunken into their heads. But dying is still a process. You're still alive while you're dying.

"It was impossible to say that we viewed our seemingly inevitable death with fear, but more correctly, with resignation," wrote Maurice. Even Maralyn, at times, was close to surrender. Survival had become their job, and she was increasingly sick of it. She consoled herself: At least they'd done more with their lives than most people.

What if one of them died, leaving the other? They discussed the possibility of the living eating the dead to stay alive. But it was only hypothetical, too appalling to plan. Instead, Maurice thought about how they could quicken things. Gassing themselves would have been peaceful, but the gas bottle was now empty. Other methods of suffocation seemed like hard work and liable to fail. He imagined simply swimming away from the raft until he drowned, but Maralyn didn't want to. She couldn't swim, after all. The struggle would be more immediate, and more violent.

"That left only the knife," wrote Maurice. But they wouldn't do it. Maralyn might be exhausted by living; she might be dying, but she wouldn't give up. She couldn't. Some vital, internal force, far deeper than intellect, or thought, or language, wouldn't let her. If she really had to die, something would have to come along and take her when she wasn't looking.

Maurice, in whom the force was less obvious, wondered if nature might resolve the question for them and send a poisonous fish into their catch.

It wasn't a fish. Maurice fell ill. The cough returned, and a fever set in. The pain in his chest became so acute he couldn't lift his arm. Maralyn tried to convince him that the pain was muscular, from when he'd pulled a large turtle on board. As the fever intensified and he could no longer move, she could see he was dangerously unwell, but wouldn't say it out loud. The truth would only deepen his depression, she felt. Instead, she encouraged him to "buck up."

Buck up. You might say it to a horse. Generations of English children have found themselves doing things they don't want to, miserably, after being told to buck up. Boys' schools and regiments, all dependent on the idea that a mood can be instructed. Maralyn called them pep talks, as if they were on the side of a football pitch and Maurice needed a shove to get him going again.

But Maurice couldn't lift himself on command. "Even Maralyn's encouraging chatter failed to raise my spirits," he wrote. His chest felt ragged from coughing. Once, in a brutal attack, he brought up something solid and viscous, a kind of bloody mucosal lump, which he thought might be part of his lung. The saltwater sores had burrowed deep into his spine, buttocks, and legs and turned into open wounds, raw and weeping. Every time a shark swam under the raft and collided with the base, he cried out in agony. There was no longer any way of sitting or lying that didn't cause savage pain. Maralyn treated the sores with antiseptic cream and tried to keep them covered with large plasters, but the plasters peeled off in the water. When she tended to the sore on his spine, which was nearly an inch wide and had tunnelled deep into his flesh, she told him it was only a small spot. He couldn't see it to check.

Maurice now lay curled up, passing in and out of consciousness. Every time he woke, Maralyn made him eat morsels of fish. She was doing all the fishing now. She was doing everything: gutting the fish, baling out and repumping the raft, killing and dissecting a turtle. "Whoopee," she called out once she'd sawed into its body, "it's full of eggs."

She passed an egg over to Maurice. A golden marble, perfectly round. He ate it, biting through the thick membrane until the yolk oozed into his mouth and stuck to his teeth and tongue like glue. He ate two more, then started to feel sick. Female turtles, they agreed, were better than the males. Packed with eggs, and their livers were larger too.

FOURTEEN

He didn't die. Failed at that, too. May turned to June. Maurice felt better.

On the first of the month, clouds rushed in and filled the sky. The wind blew from the southeast. Maurice thought the rain might miss them, but the sun fell behind a cloud. The wind dropped, then started up again from the north. A storm was coming.

Maralyn covered the books with a sail bag. Maurice fastened down the flap across the entrance. Above them, the clouds piled up on each other, multiplying, like the slow effects of an explosion. In the distance, a wall of rain glided across the surface of the ocean towards them. The wind whipped up and the first drops fell. They put on their oilskins and readied the sponges and tins for baling out. The sky darkened, as if night had fallen in a moment.

They were used to storms, to high seas and constant, insistent rain. But this was a storm that seemed to have no edge and no end. Gales battered them night after night, day after day until night and day became indistinguishable, the sky varying only in the depth of its darkness and the quantity of rain it unleashed. Squall after squall came over, howling winds tearing at the raft and stirring up the ocean. The raft felt close to giving way. In the brief moments when the rain stopped, they tried to fish. It was almost impossible to catch anything, and even if they did, there was no time to eat because the rain started pounding before they'd finished filleting.

In the tumult, the raft kept smashing into the dinghy. They were drifting so fast that Maurice made a makeshift sea anchor from some oilskin trousers to try to slow them down. When he threw them over the side tied to a rope, they quickly tangled up with the dinghy and made the raft swing round so its entrance faced the approaching waves. The fastening had come loose on the doorway; water crashed through. Maurice had to sit up and hold it closed with his hands. He could sleep only when the rain stopped.

On the morning of 5 June, the waves were so tall that they blocked out the light. It was the worst day, Maralyn noted in her diary, the coldest they'd been since leaving England. The waves came at them, one after another. Each thrust the raft upwards, then hurled it down again. The storm had gone on so long they had nothing fresh to eat, only their last tins. Maurice decided that they had to try to fish, and he climbed, precariously, from the raft to the dinghy.

"Do be careful," Maralyn yelled over the roar of the wind.

The dinghy needed baling out, but every time Maurice managed to unload some water it was struck by another wave. He kept being knocked over. "Come into the raft," shouted Maralyn. It was too dangerous. He couldn't fish properly, and what was the point of trying when there were no fish to catch? They'd retreated to the dark peace beneath the surface.

Maurice started packing the fishing gear, winding up lines and fiddling with hooks as the storm crashed around him and the waves surged beneath. At the edge of his vision he saw darkness rising behind Maralyn, more like a cliff face than water, even though it was loose with froth at its edges.

Maralyn was aware only of being lifted, up and up, until she seemed to be suspended above the ocean. When she glanced down at the dinghy below her, lodged in the middle of the wave, she saw Maurice lying on the floor, gripping the lifelines that ran along its edges. The wave was about to break. It would break, she realised, over Maurice, over the dinghy. It would swallow him whole. The drop was coming. A moment of stillness, of suspension, and then the feeling of a mountain giving way. Falling endlessly. A great, crashing gush. She saw the dinghy turn over, and Maurice disappear.

A building was collapsing on top of him. Maurice was thrust down into darkness. Under the crush of water, it felt as if he were being pushed to the bottom of the ocean. He swam frantically, no idea which way was up. Above him, suddenly, he saw the dinghy, trapping him underwater. He swam hard to the side of it, searching for its edge, and then up, fast, his head breaking the surface where he saw Maralyn, taut with panic in the raft.

He managed to reach out to her and she grabbed him, the

waves boiling around them. They were practised at dragging things out of the ocean, but Maurice was larger than a turtle. Maralyn pulled as he tried to force himself upwards, the water sucking at his body with every surge, until eventually she managed to haul him over the side, heavy as a waterlogged corpse.

~

That night, the storm still raging, they couldn't sleep. They were alive, just. Maralyn asked Maurice what would happen if the raft capsized.

Surely she could work it out for herself, he thought. It was unlike Maralyn to ask stupid questions, questions to which he could provide no satisfactory answer and for which there *was* no satisfactory answer. She would die, certainly. He would probably die too. It took a moment for compassion to sidle in. Perhaps she only needed a little reassurance.

"I don't think it will capsize, but we must prepare for that to happen," he told her. It would be difficult to turn it back over in seas like these, he added, in case Maralyn wasn't sure how slim he considered their chances.

They put the remaining tins, knives, and tin opener in the haversack, which Maralyn then tied to the raft. If the raft did overturn, at least they could salvage the bag, though it was questionable what use a tin opener would be as they were drowning.

FIFTEEN

The wind dropped, and the ocean eased in turn. The calm before a storm claims all the attention, but the calm after is just as threatening, containing, as it does, the memory of violence. Squalls kept passing over, like aftershocks.

In more peaceful water, they saw the ocean come alive again: green turtles, ridley turtles, and loggerhead turtles nearly three feet long. Petrels flew close to the water and frigate birds chased brown and blue-footed boobies until they vomited their fish, which the frigate bird would steal in midair. Sea snakes rose up to breathe at the surface. A squid landed on the raft, where it stayed until it dried out in the sun. Dolphins sometimes swam close, as did sharks, which Maralyn found unthreatening unless they arrived in a group. If Maurice made a small splash of water above them, they'd usually dart away. Once, they saw a whale shark, thirty feet long, curving its way through the water beneath them.

To cheer Maurice up, Maralyn made promises. They would catch more turtles, eat their delicious greenish fat. The sun would return. Their skin would feel warm again.

They dug through their possessions and found three more safety pins—two large, one small. Maralyn tried to bend a large one into a hook and it snapped in half. She tried again with a small one, and tied on a length of string. The triggerfish were so abundant now that they sometimes had three on the bait at once. There were spinefoot fish, too, and wolf herring, jacks, and huge dorados with bright blue-green bodies. They could fish without thinking; it was the filleting that took time and savaged their hands. Maralyn considered trailing her bleeding fingers in the water as bait.

Maurice, Maralyn noticed, let the fish swallow the hook before he caught them. He went through six or eight chunks of bait per catch. Maralyn found his method too slow, and instead waited until the fish got close, then jerked the line, which seemed to make the fish bite harder, at which point she'd quickly pull them into the dinghy. Occasionally, when they had plenty of fish to eat, she played a game with them. If she yanked hard on the line, the fish would fly across the dinghy and land in the ocean on the other side. She was sure they enjoyed it, queuing up on her side of the dinghy to take part. She couldn't help finding it fun.

Maralyn started to experiment, swishing around a length of turtle steak or shoulder bone, waiting for the fish to bite. As soon as one locked on to the flesh, she'd flip it into the dinghy.

An empty kerosene container gave her another idea. Maurice cut a square hole in its side and Maralyn threaded a line through it so she could hang the bait inside. Then she held the container's handle to lower it into the water. It took a while for the fish to approach, and at first Maralyn let them swim in and out of the container to nibble at the bait. Once they stopped darting out again, all she had to do was lift the trap out of the water and empty the fish at Maurice's feet.

The boobies, meanwhile, had taken to landing on the edge of the raft. Maurice shooed them off with a paddle. Sometimes they would land in the middle of the dinghy, digest their fish, then spatter the vessel with excrement, turning it white. Maurice, irritated, struck a booby with a paddle to make it fly away. The bird hopped into the water instead, where it regurgitated four whole flying fish, which Maurice scooped out of the water for dinner.

The boobies were so tame now, so fearless and intrusive, that it was almost inevitable they'd start killing them. The next time one landed on the raft, Maralyn grabbed its foot and Maurice wrapped it up in a towel. When they opened the towel to finish it off, the booby caught Maralyn's thumb in its beak. Maralyn wrung its neck and plucked it, and watched as its feathers were lifted into the air and scattered over the ocean.

One afternoon, Maralyn sat in the raft and watched a school of sharks pass back and forth beside her. One came close enough for her to stroke a finger along its back and feel the coarseness of its skin. When the shark turned and came back, she grabbed its tail without thinking. Maurice was asleep, so she shouted at him to wake up, then flipped the shark towards him. He caught it in a towel and wrapped it up, as he had with the booby, gripping its jaws shut. Maralyn held its tail as it squirmed.

The shark lasted for fifteen minutes before suffocating. They unwrapped the towel and looked at the dead creature. It was grey, two and a half feet long. Maurice carried it to the dinghy and cut it open. As he was gutting it, Maralyn noticed another shark swimming by and grabbed it. Maurice came back, took hold of its head, and hit it with his knife as it fought against them, then plunged the knife through its gills until it stilled. Before it had finished dying, Maralyn spotted a third shark and got hold of that one too, tugging it on board.

The sharks were now taking up quite a lot of room. The dead one was in the dinghy, the half-dead one was at their feet, and the live one was in their hands. Maurice told Maralyn to stop catching them because he had no hands or feet left to use.

Maralyn climbed into the dinghy to help him deal with them all, and they found themselves laughing, almost hysterical. They hadn't felt it for so long, the intoxication of laughter, the way it rises within, but how else could they respond to the farce and horror of all this, the realisation that, on top of everything else they'd strangled or suffocated or beheaded, they were now murdering sharks?

As they threw bits of unwanted meat into the water, a booby landed on the edge of the dinghy.

"Shall we?" said Maurice.

He grabbed it, making it squawk. Maralyn held its body, while Maurice twisted its neck. Dead within a minute. Then he caught two more.

Three sharks, three birds. They didn't particularly like the shark meat, but as they had the birds, it didn't matter. Sharks' livers and one and a half birds each. A feast.

~

After that, they took to catching the odd shark when they felt like it. Maurice was too stiff to lean far enough over the side to spot their prey, so Maralyn looked for him and told him when to reach.

One, she noticed, had particularly beautiful skin: a pearly, almost translucent grey. She cut it open and skinned it, scraping the flesh away until she was left with long sheets of clean skin, which she rolled up and placed in the corner of the dinghy to dry. She thought she might use them to make a purse.

The next day, the skin had lost its sheen. It must have been the water that made it shine. Or the presence of life, pulsing beneath. Dead and dry, it was dull and ugly.

Maralyn picked up the roll of skin and threw it back into the ocean, where it belonged.

SIXTEEN

Towards the end of June, the days became hot and steely. They caught a little turtle, seven inches long, with a shell covered in patterns. Maralyn loved it immediately, its sturdy flippers, the hopeful twists of its bald head. She told Maurice to find it a friend and he caught another, plain brown, and lobbed it into the dinghy. The pair pattered around together, climbing over Maurice and Maralyn's feet as they fished.

Conversation returned to their next boat and where they might go in it. Maurice suggested Patagonia. Maralyn wasn't sure, wondering if it might be too cold. Maurice promptly delivered a lecture explaining why he was so compelled by the place. It was one of the last remaining wildernesses, hard to navigate by boat, battered by wind, and as isolated a region as you could find. Perhaps New Zealand now seemed too tame, after months adrift. Maralyn was soon convinced. She went straight to the practicalities: how they'd anchor the boat in such wild places; what they could hunt there; what clothes they'd need.

On the last day of the month, bright and clear, they fished as usual and tipped water into the dinghy for the turtles, whom they watched splash like toddlers in a paddling pool. It had somehow become a life, what they were doing. A strange life, but a life nonetheless, with routines and habits and pets.

Not that it would last long. Maurice, now, was often on the edge of consciousness. While they still had drinkable water and were able to fish, their bodies clung to existence. But death was surely close now, hovering.

After lunch, they rested under the canopy in the raft, cooled by a southerly breeze. Everything was still, the water calm, its low, thin furrows shifting in the wind. The raft cradled them gently for once, the ocean swelling lightly beneath their bodies.

As he dozed, Maurice, so close to lapsing into darkness for good, became convinced that there was a third person in the raft. He could feel a presence, the hallucination taking solid form. He could see who it was: an American sailor called Wayne whom they'd met in Panama. In the way of dreams, he didn't wonder how or why Wayne had come to be there. He was just there. Another person, another life.

Under layers of sleep, as if drifting like a whale deep below the surface of the ocean, he sensed Maralyn somewhere far above, shaking him and calling his name.

Maurice! Maurice!

He was too far away to come back. He was so tired, so very tired, and now there was someone else to help. There was Wayne. Couldn't she leave him be? He was asleep and the sleep was thick and dark and good. He could be free.

Part Three

ONE

The *Wolmi 306* was not a beautiful ship. Paintwork that must once have gleamed white was now patchy and worn. Rust bled down her sides. She needed a rest, as did her crew, who had been at sea for two and a half years catching tuna on behalf of the *Wolmi*'s owner, the Korean Marine Industry Development Corporation.

The *Wolmi*'s captain was Suh Chong-il, a short, stocky man of thirty with a thick bowl of black hair. This was Suh's first voyage as skipper, and it had been an unambiguous failure. Early on, an accident on board had killed one of his crew. Later, the ship had been so badly damaged in a violent storm that they'd had to change their course and anchor for repairs. By the end of June 1973, the crew were exhausted, desperate to return to their families.

Suh didn't blame them. Two and a half years was a long time

to be at sea, in a relentless and womanless routine of catching and storing skipjack, yellowfin, and bigeye tuna, as well as cooking, cleaning, and the endless maintenance required as the ocean does its work and the ship gradually surrenders itself to rust.

~

Early on the morning of 30 June, Suh noticed four seagulls following the boat. A sign of "something evil, according to the Korean superstition," he wrote later. It wasn't unusual for gulls to gather round a fishing boat, hoping to swoop on its catch. Signs tend to reveal themselves only in retrospect.

Mid-afternoon, the chief deck man, Kim Min-chan, knocked on Suh's cabin door. He'd seen an object in the water two miles off the starboard side and wanted Suh to come and have a look. Up on deck, Suh saw something, too, but it was too far away to say what it was with any certainty. From here it resembled a black spot, appearing and disappearing as the waves rose and fell.

Suh ordered his men to ignore the sighting and carry on, but his gaze kept being drawn back to the spot. There it was, there it wasn't, bobbing up and down. Maybe it was another fishing boat. For some reason, he couldn't quite let it go. Out here in the Pacific, where there was nothing, there was something. He wanted to know what it was. He ordered his men to turn the ship around.

As they approached, the spot became a shape. Two shapes.

Two vessels, tied together. Closer still, and they saw a body, then two bodies. They were moving, these bodies, but they hardly looked human. Suh could just about tell they were a man and a woman. The man's gaunt face was half covered by a thick beard. The woman had long, ragged hair, and legs that looked as fragile and thin as willow branches. They appeared ancient and so emaciated he could see the shape of their bones beneath their skin. He was near enough now to see their dark and hollowed eyes, fixed on the boat as though it might disappear if they looked away.

Suh ordered the crew to pull alongside. His men threw ropes over the starboard side. As the ropes swung above the dinghy, Suh watched the man claw at the air, unable to grab hold of the ends. When he eventually caught one, he didn't seem to know what to do with it. The crew shouted instructions, and eventually he managed to wedge the rope's knotted end into the rowlock of the dinghy. The men pulled the dinghy close to their boat and dropped a ladder down.

Suh told his men to help them up. The man wanted the woman to go first, but the ladder was nearer the dinghy and the crew insisted that he go up instead. Suh watched as he clung to the ladder, his spindly arms heaving his body up and over the side. Once on deck, he could neither stand nor sit, but fell forward onto his hands and knees like a dog.

The crew pulled the raft along until it was beneath the ladder, and the woman followed. It seemed impossible that her legs could support her weight, but her eyes were locked ahead, determination hardening her face as she climbed.

Once they were on deck, Suh could examine them. Their clothes were rotten, barely covering their bodies. A fungus was growing all over the man's skin, livid and red. They both stank.

Suh panicked. They were surely diseased. The last thing he needed was an infection to spread among his crew. He instructed his men to lay out a blanket on the far side of the deck. They led the couple over to it, supporting their weight from either side, until they lowered them down and their bodies collapsed like animals shot in the legs. The cook, Jun Sang-won, brought them each a glass of milk. They thanked him profusely, and sipped. The woman began to cry.

All their belongings were still floating on the water below. Suh felt that he couldn't leave them there, so he told his crew to haul everything on board. Piece by piece, they brought up the life raft, the dinghy, the oar, the chart, the logbook, the diary, the dictionaries, knives, spoons, three bowls, a manicure set, electric wire, a first-aid kit, a packet of pills, eight plastic cans filled with stale water, and another plastic container packed with rotting meat. *Everything* stank.

Suh wasn't sure where to start. There was no protocol for this, though the stench seemed to suggest itself as a priority. He couldn't take them down to a cabin yet. Any infection would spread more quickly in the closed world of the ship below deck. On the port side of the deck was a hose. That would do. He asked them to move over towards it, but they didn't respond. Perhaps they didn't understand. "When I shouted again," wrote Suh, "they began to crawl slowly like babies."

Six crew hosed down the man, as if he were a horse after a race. The woman was taken to one side, for privacy. Kim, the chief deck man, helped her wash with a bucket. Clean trousers and shirts were brought up for them to wear, clothes that the crew had bought as presents for their families. "Dressed in new clothes the couple looked more like humans," wrote Suh, "but their elbows and knees protruded so much that they looked like a dead man's arms and legs." The reek of their old clothes was so appalling that the men threw them back into the ocean.

Once they'd returned to their blanket, Suh watched the woman pat dry her hair, a practised gesture she must have performed a thousand times in the comfort of a bedroom. She crawled over to their heap of things and dug out a comb. Sitting close to the man, she started combing his hair, then stroked his cheek.

The crew fell quiet. Suh felt a pain in his chest, which he decided was heartache. Perhaps it was the years away from home, the years without touch or intimacy, the sight of a wife's kindness, a small but deliberate act of care. He hadn't seen or felt anything like it for so long. It must have been this tenderness, he thought, that had kept them alive.

~

Suh would have to tell the ship's company about the rescue. They'd want to know who the couple were. You can't just pick up a pair of strangers from the ocean and expect no questions. He was worried they were Russian, which would go down badly. He couldn't have Communists on board.

Suh found the passports among their things, damp and tattered. Maurice Charles Bailey and Maralyn Collins Bailey. Aged forty and thirty-two. Unbelievable. They looked decades older, the man especially.

He assigned them a cabin near a bathroom and ordered his men to take the mattresses from the beds and put them on the floor. They clearly weren't strong enough to climb up to the bunks.

Later, when he went down to talk to them, he found them chatting with his men, their spirits high. Automatically respectful of the skipper's presence, they tried to sit up, but he told them to lie back down, and asked how they were feeling. "Fine, fine," they replied, which couldn't possibly be true.

They seemed so eager to please. They weren't Russian, they promised, but English. Their boat had sunk on their way to the Galápagos. When they told him where exactly, he calculated that they'd drifted nine hundred miles northwest of their course. It was pure chance that they'd been spotted. The question was what he should *do* with them. The *Wolmi* was nearing the end of her voyage. His crew wanted to get home to South Korea. He didn't want to have to stop or divert their course. Perhaps Mr. and Mrs. Bailey, this strange, primeval pair, could come too. They were his now, like cargo. He'd got much of his captaincy wrong so far, but at least the task in front of him was clear. Here were two sick people, closer to death than life: He had to look after them.

~

Suh summoned the ship's engineer, Pae Sok-dong, who had served in the medical corps of the South Korean army. The man had to be dealt with first. Whatever ailment was plaguing his skin needed attention. When they gingerly turned him over and saw the state of his buttocks, eaten away by infected, suppurating sores, they had to look away. There was hardly anything left.

One of the largest sores was covered with a patch fixed by adhesive tape. Pae tried to remove the patch, but every time he pulled, the tape began tearing off the remaining shreds of skin. He had to slap the side of the buttock to distract the poor man, who was shaking and moaning from the pain. It took twenty minutes to get the tape off, skin disintegrating as he tugged. Underneath, Pae found a small crater, brimming with pus. He pressed out the ooze and a deep hole opened up; he could see straight through to the bone. Pae applied antiseptic ointment, and covered it again.

That they were both chronically malnourished was obvious, but Suh knew that he had to limit what they ate, at least at first. Too much too soon would make them ill. He instructed Jun, the ship's cook, to create a special menu. He'd give up any treats that were his due as captain, and his men would go without extras, so that the couple could have a familiar and varied diet: chicken, beef, eggs, bread, watermelon, pineapple.

~

That night, Suh couldn't sleep. He left Pae to keep watch outside their room, in case the couple lapsed into a sudden decline. Even so, he worried they wouldn't survive.

At around midnight, they came out of their cabin. Somehow,

they dragged themselves up on deck, and Suh watched them hobble across to the handrail, holding on to each other for support. Standing at the edge, they looked out to sea.

"I thought I could understand them," Suh wrote later. Understand, that is, why they wanted to get out of bed in the middle of the night, barely able to walk, their bodies still exhausted and in pain, in order to stare at the black ocean, cold and hostile in the dark, an ocean that had nearly claimed their lives. Until that morning, it had been their home.

TWO

The milk wasn't fresh, how could it be, out here in the middle of the ocean? No, the milk came in tins and packets of powder from a factory in the Netherlands and was stored in bulk in the galley. When it was brought to them as they sat on the blanket, newly aboard the ship that had come to their rescue, Maralyn tried to do what was right, what was polite, what she had been raised to do, and express her thanks. But it was difficult amid the rush of taste and the knowledge of safety, the presence of other human beings and their gentle attention, to keep herself from crying.

~

Maurice hadn't believed Maralyn when she'd told him the ship was coming. He'd sworn under his breath at being woken and forced himself to his knees. He couldn't see a thing. She must have been mistaken, imagining things. More wild fantasies. They hadn't seen a ship for forty-three days.

"It's there, behind you!" Maralyn shouted.

She was right. She was *always right.* There it was: a small white ship, striped with rust. Even then, he was convinced it hadn't seen them. He told her to stop waving and save her strength. He couldn't bear to watch her, shouting into the breeze. Let it go on, he thought. This is our world now, on the water, among the birds and the turtles and the fish. This is where we belong.

And then it turned. He saw shapes moving on deck. It was coming back for them. "You've found us a ship!" he said, as if she had fished it out of the sea.

They were both naked, and suddenly aware of their nakedness. "Sort some clothes out, quickly," he shouted. His captain's voice.

Maralyn found them damp shorts and rotting shirts which they pulled on as the ship drew alongside. They saw, up on deck, a group of bewildered men. Human faces. They remembered, before they climbed up the ladder one by one, to release their pair of pet turtles back into the ocean.

~

It was all they had imagined for four months. So many ships had gone past that the sight had become something between a joke and an insult. Now a ship had turned. In hindsight, every bloody cough, every beheaded turtle, every rush of diarrhoea, seemed to contain purpose, a sense of leading somewhere. An ending that wasn't death.

And yet, even in the moment of rescue, Maurice felt that weightless sensation of something passing; something precious and unrepeatable, something you could recognise as such only once it was safely over. There had been a strange kind of peace adrift on the ocean, even if it was a peace close to annihilation.

As usual, their gaze seemed to point in opposite directions, his backwards, hers relentlessly forwards. Sitting on the blanket, milk-drunk, surrounded by the crew, they turned to each other.

"We've made it," said Maurice.

"Now for *Auralyn II*, and Patagonia!" Maralyn replied, as if they could set off tomorrow.

~

But this milk: It was the finest they'd ever tasted, warm and thick and sweet. Like newborns, their bodies seemed to know that milk was the first requirement. They drank whole glasses of it in single gulps.

After that, they were left alone to eat, as if the crew knew how significant an experience it must be. Early on, one of the men took a photograph of them during a meal, sitting next to each other at a table. Their expressions were so grave they looked as if they were locked in prayer.

Their first meal was simple. Eggs, bread, corned beef. But even so. Eggs, cooked and warm. Bread spread with butter.

Corned beef, a child's food, salty and thick. Afterwards, they drank water, clean water that was neither contaminated nor flavoured by rubber. They sucked it down and asked for more, then more again. It seemed they could have as much of it as they wanted.

As well as food and water, the men gave them vitamins, toothbrushes, and toothpaste. "Kindness itself," Maralyn wrote in her diary. Their bodies, sensing safety, stopped pretending to function. Their legs began to swell, oedemas forming from fluid retention, a symptom of starved bodies. They could hardly move. But down in their cabin, both able to lie at full stretch for the first time in months, they were elated.

When Suh came down, Maurice tried to congratulate him, one skipper to another, on spotting them in the emptiness of the ocean, but Suh didn't seem to understand what he was saying. Maurice gave up, presuming his Derby accent was the problem. For some reason, Maralyn found it easier to make herself understood.

In the morning, Pae gave them a bucket to wash in. Jun brought them more milk. Maralyn asked Suh if he'd tried it, eager for him not to miss the extraordinary experience. No, replied Suh. "Is it because you're short of milk?" she asked, worried they were taking more than their fair share. No, said Suh. He just didn't like it. He didn't need to like it.

~

Soon enough, their days on the *Wolmi* found a rhythm. They woke early and went out on deck to see the sun rise, supporting each other, clinging to the handrails, dragging themselves if necessary. Dawn, they told Suh, had been their favourite time on the raft. It always offered fresh hope. Maybe today would be the day.

Then breakfast, a snack, lunch, another snack, tea, dinner. The day was measured out in meals. And milk. Breakfast was fried eggs, bread and butter, milk. Lunch: fried onions, onion and mushroom soup, four rolls, four eggs, and milk. Tea: biscuits and milk. Dinner: onion and mushroom soup, four rolls, four eggs, corned beef. More milk. Maralyn wrote down every meal in her diary as if she had to see it on the page to believe it. They were so full they saved a roll, an egg, and some onions for a "midnight feast."

Between meals, Maurice lay on his bed, motionless, but Maralyn was busy, copying out her diary into a new notebook. Pae kept having to tell her to rest. Her legs were still swollen. She needed to lie down. But there were things to do, as always. They insisted on going to the toilet without any help. "Leave us alone so that we can learn to walk by ourselves," they told the crew, as they crawled.

The men visited regularly. Pae came frequently to treat Maurice's sores with ointment and to massage Maralyn's legs. Every time, he made a point of noticing an improvement: Their colour had come back; they were putting on weight. He thought of his encouragement as a kind of psychotherapy. Tell them they're getting better, and they will.

Suh kept giving them things: A tub of moisturiser he'd been taking home to his sister. A chocolate bar and chewing gum. A notebook, pens, and paper. The rest of the crew brought them presents, too: belts to hold up their overlarge trousers, a box of Milk Tray. "Tasted v. good," noted Maralyn. Seeing how they liked to go out on deck and look at the ocean, some of the men made a seat with a canopy over the top so that they could sit sheltered from the sun.

After so long alone, Maurice and Maralyn found themselves overwhelmed by such generosity. "As our voyage continued, we began to feel as though we belonged to that ship," wrote Maurice. It was like being part of a family. When Suh proposed that they travel with them to South Korea, Maurice and Maralyn were delighted. It wasn't as if they had anywhere else to go.

~

On 3 July, their fourth day on board, Suh decided it was time for some photographs. The crew carried Maurice and Maralyn's remaining possessions out on deck, reinflated the raft and the dinghy, and arranged various containers and buckets and bottles in front, like unearthed treasure.

Maurice and Maralyn stood in the middle, as if in a wedding photograph, with the crew arranged around them. Maurice clutched one of the dinghy's oars with his right hand and Maralyn with his left. They tilted towards each other, as if the gentlest push might collapse them in on themselves. One of the men wedged himself in the doorway of the raft's cover. He seemed to fill the entire craft. The rest stood solemnly round the edges in white shirts and vests. Only Maurice and Maralyn smiled—the tired, patient smiles of people for whom smiling was still an effort. Afterwards, the crew poured out all the old rainwater from the containers, rain that had taken Maurice and Maralyn hours of storms and squalls to collect drip by drip in the bucket on the raft. The smell of the water as it ran across the deck was appalling. At the sight of it dribbling away, down the side of the ship and back into the ocean, water into water, Maralyn's eyes filled with tears. All that work.

THREE

Word of the rescue spread in South Korea. On 4 July, a telegram arrived over the *Wolmi*'s radio receiver, noted down by Pok, the radio officer. There were eight questions from the *Hankook Ilbo* and *The Korea Times*, requesting more information about this mysterious English couple. Where had they come from and where were they going? What had *happened*?

Suh couldn't answer them. He'd been so preoccupied with keeping Maurice and Maralyn alive he'd forgotten to ask them how they had come to be adrift in the first place. He rushed down to their cabin and told them of the newspapers' interest. "People were genuinely interested. *In us!*" wrote Maurice. It seemed absurd.

Suh went through the questions, Pae made notes, and Suh wrote up a detailed report that he sent to the papers and his company. He'd been nervous about how his employers might react, but they replied with a congratulatory telegram. At last, an achievement.

His only achievement, Suh reflected. If he hadn't found Maurice and Maralyn, he'd have written the whole voyage off as a calamity. Even then, finding them had seemed like only another event, one of the endless strange and unpredictable things that happen at sea. But now that the press was interested, Suh began to reassess the rescue. It seemed to mean something to people.

The first article appeared on 5 July in *The Korea Times*: KOREAN VESSEL SAVES DRIFTING BRITISH COUPLE. Five brief paragraphs, full of errors. "The couple, identified as M. C. Bailey, 41, and his wife, were said to have been drifting aboard their yacht, whose engine had developed trouble." No whale, no sinking, no raft; Maralyn wasn't even named.

Soon after, there were more telegrams, mostly from South Korea. The next day, another story ran in *The Korea Times*. The yacht had sunk, they'd been adrift for 117 days, they'd nearly died of starvation. All broadly true, but they called Maurice "Michael" and Maralyn was still unmentioned beyond being his wife.

Yet more telegrams arrived, from Britain and America. The *Daily Mail*, *Sunday Times*, *Sunday People*, *Daily Mirror*, and *Daily Express* wanted details. Pok stayed up all night collating them. In the morning, Suh went back to Maurice and Maralyn and showed them some of the messages. "Mr. and Mrs. Bailey," he told them, "you are a world sensation!"

Maurice and Maralyn couldn't understand. In their minds, they had existed uncomfortably on a raft and a dinghy for nearly four months, an extraordinary experience for *them* but surely not of much significance to anyone else.

The papers made offers for an exclusive: the *Daily Mail*, £6,000; the *Daily Express*, £6,500. Maurice and Maralyn had calculated that once they were back in England, it would take them eight years to earn enough money to fund their next boat. If they sold their story, they could start building it straightaway.

Maurice replied to each offer: We'll consider it. He was no fool. He realised that they had a commodity whose value would only increase the more people wanted it. They'd hold out.

~

A message came through from the Korean Marine Industry Development Corporation on 8 July. Pok, keeping vigil by his radio, woke Suh at three in the morning to relay it. The *Wolmi* was to stop at Honolulu, the next major port, for Maurice and Maralyn to be checked by doctors. South Korea was too far, and the corporation had to be sure the couple were recovering as they should be. The world's media was watching; the value of their cargo had substantially increased.

Suh knew that his crew, wishing for home, would be crushed. He'd envisaged sailing into Busan, crowds cheering, his prize catch on board. There seemed little chance that Maurice and Maralyn, once lodged in the luxury of a plush Hawaiian hotel, would want to get back on board the *Wolmi*.

Suh told Maurice and Maralyn of the decision. "We know our own health," said Maralyn, defiantly, though Maurice now had infections in his finger and ear and was complaining of headaches. Suh explained about his company's concerns and they gave in. Maurice promised that as soon as the medical checks were complete, they would return to the ship.

~

On 13 July, the sun rose into mist. Suh was on the bridge. Maurice and Maralyn stood alongside him, holding hands. In the haze, uncertain shapes, blue against the sky, formed and dissolved. What might have been a cloud darkened and hardened on the horizon. They saw the jagged edges of peaks and the pleated slopes of mountains. Blue turned to green, lush and tropical; the green of fern-rich forests, pines, and fruit trees heavy with papaya, breadfruit, and mango, of monkeypod and umbrella trees, tamarind and kukui nut, avocado and kiawe. Green spotted with the colour of bougainvillea and hibiscus.

"Is that really Hawaii?" Maralyn asked Suh, as if disbelieving that such a place could actually exist.

The island of Oahu assembled itself before them. The dark, creviced faces of Diamond Head rose up from the ocean. Curved strips of golden beach edged the landmass. The Pacific glinted in the sun as they approached the shore, confirming the presence, according to local myth, of fairies who fished off the coast of Waialua. Beyond, the tall buildings of Honolulu jutted against the sky. A city, fixed in its position, can appear so arrogant after a long time at sea.

A speedboat carved through the water to meet them. A helicopter circled above, a pulsing roar. Both full of newsmen, Suh assumed, wanting a first sight of the English couple, plucked from the ocean.

FOUR

Hawaii, in 1973, was a building site. Cranes bent over their work, constructing rows of luxury hotels. Every day, Pan Am and United aircraft ejected hot squads of tourists from the mainland, determined to holiday. The place was a rich man's playground, the guidebooks said: the most expensive resort in the world!

Along Waikiki Beach, the hotel rooms had balconies from which guests could watch the waving palms on the beach and the surfers rising and falling on the long, slim rollers formed by the contours of the ocean floor, their heads dotting the water like seals. Harried New York businessmen could unbutton stiff collars and put on shorts, while their wives tried on bright, new bikinis. Before long, they'd be wearing their beachwear around town without a thought, on their way to watch dancing girls with flowers in their hair. Later, over cocktails by a pool, they'd let the drink dissolve their former selves.

On 13 July, as the *Wolmi* docked at Pier 8 in the port of Honolulu, Maurice and Maralyn arranged themselves against the guardrail on deck, left arms bent and propped on the rail, right arms aloft, hands flapping. They smiled broadly; synchronised wavers. Maurice wore shorts and a white T-shirt with striped cuffs; Maralyn an A-line skirt and floral shirt, with a thick cardigan over the top. Her hair was tied back, but it kept coming loose in the breeze and blowing across her face. At the harbour, Suh estimated that there were a hundred reporters and cameramen jostling for space. Maurice smartened up, changing into a fresh white shirt and dark trousers. Maralyn took off her cardy and tamed her hair. As they hobbled down the gangway, their legs still felt as if they might collapse beneath them. Maralyn went first, with Suh's men in front and behind, holding her hands. She stared at her feet in concentration. After a few steps, she was able to reach the ropes on the sides and clutched them to guide her down. Maurice shuffled after her, wincing in pain. Finally, they reached hard, flat ground. The uncompromising certainty of land. Their bodies lurched.

And *bang*! They were surrounded. Photographers elbowed one another in competition to get a shot, cameras clacked, reporters yelled questions. The Korean Consul General Lee Kew-sung and British Consul General D. G. Barr came forward, in suits and ties, to greet them. Officialdom had been busy, sensing opportunity. A welcome ceremony had been arranged. Barr handed Suh a formal letter of appreciation on behalf of the British government, and thanked the crew for rescuing this pair of British citizens, as if the end of their ordeal were the resolution of a prolonged diplomatic crisis. Two Korean girls, representative of the Korean community in Hawaii, hung leis around their necks.

Suh guided Maurice and Maralyn through the crowd. Immediately, they were like children again, no longer in control of their movements. Someone else had done the organising, the cars, the itinerary; they would be told what to do and where to go. The first obligation was a reception and press conference at the Korean consulate. The television crews, Maurice was informed, were already set up, the room rammed with expectant reporters.

Maurice and Maralyn were taken to the front and sat down behind a row of tables, facing banks of unknown faces and cameras. Why were they taking so many pictures? wondered Maurice. What was there to see? Maralyn politely smiling and Maurice wiping his brow, looking hot and anxious. No one could hear them properly as they asked the Korean journalists to convey their gratitude to the people of Korea for saving their lives. The press hadn't come for gratitude. They wanted to know about the whale. Was it a killer whale? Had they nearly died? Had they found God?

Had they found *God*? Maurice was incensed. It was obviously nobody's business whether they'd found God or not, and in any case what a lazy assumption, that an experience such as theirs should lead to some kind of divine epiphany. How patronising, really, to think they required the intervention of a supernatural being to survive when their survival had been achieved through graft and wits and endurance and luck. This God you put so much faith in, thought Maurice, was the same God, by logical extension, that made the men who injured the whale who'd sunk them in the first place. Couldn't they see it made no sense? And of course it wasn't a killer whale. He knew a sperm whale when he saw one.

The journalists wouldn't have it. "It did attack you after all," said one, "so it must have been a killer!" The sloppiness of it all. "They were using the noun inadvisably," wrote Maurice, "not as a branch of the cetacean order but in an adjectival sense such as might be applied to an antisocial class of man." Why couldn't people be precise?

Something was slipping out of his grasp, their story already being misconstrued. They'd only just come ashore and it felt as if what had happened to them were no longer theirs.

Maurice tried to straighten out the facts. He explained how they'd caught sharks and how Maralyn had been better at fishing than him. He defended their killing of sea creatures: He knew it was wrong, but they did it to stay alive. He told them that thirst had worried them more than hunger, that the storms had been frightening, especially when waves loomed over the raft. And he spoke, too, of how he'd struggled. "Only the tenacity of my wife kept me alive," he told the reporters. His impression of their roles had solidified into fact. He had given up; she had kept them going.

But as he tried to explain what had happened, Maurice realised that nothing he said came close to the truth. He could describe how they made the fishhooks, or cut up the turtles, but that didn't bear any relation to how filleting the fish or eating turtle fat had actually felt. How could anyone who hadn't known what they'd known possibly understand?

Facts alone couldn't communicate the interior experience of being alone for so long in the blankness of the ocean, out of time, the only structure the rising and setting of the sun. Nor could they say what it felt like to starve, to assume you would never see another human being again, to know you were dying. Maurice felt tired.

Still, he did most of the talking. Maralyn, according to one reporter, "smiled shyly by his side," as Maurice explained how she had taken charge. "She worked harder and shamed me into doing things," said Maurice. "She did not bully, she did it by example."

When Maralyn did speak, she downplayed the hardships. "The only thing wrong with me is a wound I got when a seagull attacked me," the *Daily Mirror* reported, as if the weeks of starvation had had no effect.

Another journalist asked her if she'd follow her husband to sea again. "The small brunette said 'of course,'" reported *The Korea Times*.

The small brunette. "Of course."

Would she *follow* her husband? For a start, he had followed *her*.

~

Fifteen minutes of questions, and the press conference was over. Maurice and Maralyn were driven to the Sheraton Waikiki, a new five-star hotel overlooking the beach. As guests of the management, they'd been given a penthouse suite at the top of one of a pair of curved thirteen-story towers, joined in the middle like the wings of a bird.

Alone for the first time since they'd boarded the *Wolmi*, they stood together on their balcony, looking out to sea. The beach was scattered with people. Palm trees tilted and stretched in the breeze. The waves rolled in, white edged and curling, as if they knew that their reputation as the world's finest had to be maintained. From the thirteenth floor, the ocean seemed distinct and separate. They saw it how other people see it, as scenery or playground.

In the freshly made bed, clean sheets, a solid base, they slept their first night on land. Nothing moved. They were being held up by foundations dug deep into the earth and their bodies knew it. Muscles knotted for five months could finally soften.

In the morning, Maurice rang reception and tried to order room service. The American woman who answered his call couldn't make out what he was saying. "I'm sorry, sir," she said, "but we don't speak Japanese."

Maurice, once again, was unintelligible, as if he spoke a different language from everyone else on Earth.

~

The British consulate sent its doctors. Reports were good. Their teeth were in poor shape, but their digestion appeared back to normal and Maurice's skin fungus had almost disappeared.

They were exhausted and lacking energy, but that would come back. Their bodies would take weeks and months to fully regain their strength.

After the press conference, British and Korean newspapers ran the story over the weekend of 14 and 15 July. Maurice and Maralyn were emblazoned across the front pages of the *Sunday People* (MY WIFE SAVED US, SAYS SEA ORDEAL MAN) and the *Sunday Mirror* (THE SAFETY PIN MIRACLE) next to a photograph of them with leis around their necks, smiling wanly.

On 18 July, *The Korea Times* and *Hankook Ilbo* published the first instalment of a thirteen-part account of the rescue written by Captain Suh: SAVING SPARK OF HUMAN LIFE BRINGS SURGE OF EXCITEMENT. Suh wrote of the moment of rescue and the sight and stench of the half-dead couple with intense feeling: "June 30, 1973, has become the most unforgettable day in my 30-year life." If it had not been for the Baileys, he added, the voyage would have been a bitter memory.

British regional papers from Bristol to Aberdeen covered the story. The *Derby Evening Telegraph*, proud of its connection to "the former Allestree couple," included an excerpt of Maralyn's first phone call to Ada from their hotel room. "You shouldn't have worried," Maralyn reportedly told her mother. "Maurice and I are like two bad pennies. We always turn up in the end."

In one of the reports, Maralyn claimed that she and Maurice hadn't argued, too busy fishing and trying to stay alive to fight. Unlike Maurice, only too willing to trawl back over his weaknesses, Maralyn was already painting over the cracks. She seemed to want to give an impression of uncorrupted resilience. They'd survived, hadn't they? Why dwell on the problems?

After sifting through all the offers from the British papers, they decided to sell their full account to the *Daily Express* for £10,000. An extraordinary sum. The *Express* was impatient to publish, however, and sent a journalist couple from Los Angeles, Ivor and Sally Davis, to interview them.

The Davises spent several days with Maurice and Maralyn, holed up in their hotel suite. Ivor spoke to Maurice and tried, at times with difficulty, to extract a more intimate, personal story. Sally, meanwhile, took Maralyn into another room, in the hope that she might speak more freely. The results were articles written in Maurice and Maralyn's names, published over several days in the *Express*, which proclaimed the series "the greatest survival story of them all." NEVER HAVE TWO PEOPLE DEPENDED SO MUCH ON EACH OTHER, ran the headline. WHEN HE FALTERED HER COURAGE SUSTAINED HIM. In the photograph, an awkward shot, Maralyn is shown leaning over Maurice having his leg treated while sprawled sideways on a mattress.

At first, Maralyn's writing maintained the note form of her diary entries. After an account of *Auralyn*'s sinking, she reverted to a kind of shorthand. "No ships"; "Electrical storm"; "Made paper dominoes from notepaper and played." But then, drawn out by Sally, her tone became more confessional. She described Maurice's depressions and self-blame. "M keeps insisting he's a miserable failure but I keep telling him again and again that we are still alive and we have done so much together, enough to fill three lifetimes," she wrote.

All marriages have their repeated conversations. They'd had this one for four months: his despair, her resolution. As she described the pep talks she gave him, the plans for the new boat, and the dinner parties they'd have on board, she came to a stark conclusion: "I discover that men may be physically the stronger of the sexes but mentally women are tops."

Maurice's version of events was published the day after Maralyn's. From the start he made his theme clear: The entire impetus for the trip had come from Maralyn, and once the boat had sunk, she was in charge. "I saw that she was stronger and more capable than I was and I sat back and was prepared to let her take over. And she did."

As a consequence, their marriage was more equal, he concluded. His wife was not only more able but more disciplined. She could take a tin of food and eat it slowly, spoonful by spoonful, even when starving. "If it had been just me, I'd have wolfed it down." She had become the adult, in a way, and he the child. "She may secretly have been pleased that I wavered and she took command," he added, almost in passing.

Maurice might never have seen his debilitating self-doubt as a gift, but it had given Maralyn power.

~

In Honolulu, everyone wanted a turn with them. The Daughters of the British Empire invited them to a special event, which Maurice took pleasure in refusing. A group who believed they were the Hawaiian wing of the Bailey family also laid claim.

Maurice ignored them. The consul's wife took Maurice and Maralyn in hand.

There were lunches and dinners and drinks, picnics on Diamond Head overlooking the ocean. They watched a hula dance and were taken on tours of a pineapple plantation, coastal blowholes, and Pearl Harbor. Maralyn politely noted every event in her diary, the "beautiful house" of one couple, the "very good buffet meal" at a party. Her entries were short, single lines, as if she didn't have the energy to recall details. At one dinner, she wrote, they "could hardly keep awake."

At an event for medical students in the university amphitheatre, they were invited onstage to discuss the physical feat of their survival, stunning the audience when they revealed they'd eaten triggerfish, always assumed to be poisonous, for weeks on end.

One bright, windy day, they had their photograph taken sitting on a wall high up above the Punchbowl, a vast volcanic crater formed by lava bursting through ancient coral reefs that now housed a huge cemetery for American war veterans, each marked by a flat granite headstone. From above, they looked like the long, dotted lines of road markings.

They were getting better at photos now. Their smiles seemed genuine, the muscles in their faces a little more relaxed. It looked like a typical holiday snap, except this wasn't a holiday. It was hard to know quite what it was, or who they were now, come to that. They seemed to be somewhere between tourists and celebrities, being shown things and being shown off, as much of an attraction as anything they saw.

~

Another decision arrived from the Korean Marine Industry Development Corporation. Maurice and Maralyn's health was too fragile for another long journey at sea. Suh and his crew, waiting on the *Wolmi* without visas, and so only able to step on land under escort, would have to sail home to South Korea without them.

"The disappointment to us was considerable," wrote Maurice. "We longed to be aboard and to share once more in the life of that ship." They would follow as soon as they could, he promised. The South Korean government was enthusiastic to have them. Their rescue was now internationally renowned. By hosting Maurice and Maralyn, it could show off South Korea to the world.

An official came to visit them in the hotel and told them that a Korean newspaper, *Dong-A Ilbo*, the Korean embassy, and Korean Air had come together to organise the trip. Everything was arranged.

It was all well and good, but Maurice wanted to be back on the *Wolmi*. He missed its rituals; a strict and limited timetable on repeat. Land, so far, had been overwhelming in its variety and demands. Too many people, too much attention. At sea, they'd be alone again. But it seemed they were no longer in a position to decide how their lives would unfold. It wasn't just a lack of home or income, aside from the *Daily Express*'s unlikely cheque. Their future was blank, apart from the promise of a boat yet to be built.

As the *Wolmi* sailed out of port, shrinking until she was only a mark on the horizon, Maurice and Maralyn waved and shouted after her in Korean. Goodbye and good luck!

The crew would all be in their positions. Suh on the bridge, Jun in the galley, Pok at the radio. Everything as it always was, except for the absence of an English couple, slowly returning to life.

FIVE

On 1 August, Maurice and Maralyn boarded a plane to Seoul, and flew over the great blue plain of the Pacific Ocean in a single day.

The crowd awaiting them at Gimpo airport was not quite as devoted as the one that had welcomed Billy Graham a few weeks before. The American evangelist had preached the Gospel to more than a million people on the mile-long plaza on the island of Yeouido in the Han River and ended his sermon to the gathering with an instruction: "If you're willing to forsake all other gods, stand up." One by one they rose, before Graham climbed into a waiting helicopter and flew off.

Maurice, who had long ago forsaken all gods, disembarked from the plane first, wearing a brown shirt and tightly belted trousers, both hanging loose on his still-thin frame. He carried a leather bag and gripped the handrail as he grinned at the cameras.

Maralyn followed, in a loud floral shirt, white trousers, white sandals. She looked down at her feet, as if worried about falling. "We are very, very happy," Maurice told the reporters, in case their smiles weren't convincing. As they emerged from the airport into the warm night of the city, reporters and photographers swarmed around them. Two hundred of them, according to the *Dong-A Ilbo*. Security guards had to hustle them through the throng to a waiting black limousine. A police escort drove off in front, and the reporters chased behind as they sped to their hotel, the Sejong, in the heart of Seoul. The plan was to lose the press on the way so that they couldn't find out where Maurice and Maralyn were staying. But it all seemed a little pointless, thought Maurice, when they arrived at the hotel to find a large banner strung up over the entrance: WELCOME TO KOREA, MR. AND MRS. BAILEY!

The Sejong had opened only a few years earlier, named after the fourth king of the Joseon dynasty. Its name blazed in lights above the top row of windows. Facing it was the wooded mountain of Namsan, from which a newly built communications tower rose into the sky.

This time, their suite was decorated in traditional Korean style. Maurice liked it. This was how he'd imagined South Korea, unlike the Seoul he'd seen through the limousine windows as they drove from the airport. He'd expected traditional, wooden houses with upturned, tiled roofs. Instead, they'd passed skyscrapers, elevated highways, and brightly lit supermarkets. Under the authoritarian leadership of Park Chung-hee, South Korea was in its first flush of industrial expansion, building over the ruins of the Korean War. Maurice was disappointed. It looked more like an American city than the Korea he'd had in mind.

~

Once again, the invitations descended. They had no choice. Maurice and Maralyn, newly appointed mascots of the country, were in South Korea to be photographed doing everything they were asked. Cameras surrounded them as the mayor of Seoul, Yang Taek-sik, presented them with a golden key to the city and an honorary citizenship certificate. There were lunches with the British ambassador, dinners with the heads of TV studios.

When their pictures appeared in the paper, their names were often wrongly assigned in the captions: Maurice for Maralyn, Maralyn for Maurice.

Maurice struggled, at times, to find his way. At a dinner with twenty businessmen, they were served by *gisaeng*, once courtesans employed to entertain men of the higher classes, now women who performed the role for visitors. They glided around the floor in traditional Korean dress, hair piled on their heads, and placed a bottle of whisky next to each guest. Maurice and Maralyn declined, so no one else drank either. Maurice assumed he'd spoilt the evening and wanted to leave, but the dinner never seemed to end. Hours after the meal was over, still no one left. He wondered how they could escape. Eventually, one of the men rose to his feet and they all fled. Only later did it emerge that they had all been waiting for Maurice, the chief guest, to depart first.

Still, Maralyn noted in her diary, there had been some good folk dancing.

~

To start their official tour, a fast train carried them east through the Korean countryside to see South Korea's finest achievements. At the new Hyundai shipyard on the east coast near Ulsan, Maurice was impressed, as he was required to be, by the sight of vast ships being built at a speed that no European yard could hope to emulate.

They crossed the country north to south, east to west, stopping at a Buddhist monastery in the mountains of the southern provinces. The monks wanted photos with them. At Panmunjom, where the armistice was signed at the end of the war in 1953, they were saluted by a guard of honour, as if they were heads of state on a diplomatic mission rather than a married couple who'd spent four months on a life raft. As they were shown round and taken to the barbed-wire border with North Korea, Maurice was told not to wave in case the harmless gesture was misinterpreted as an act of war.

At last the *Wolmi* arrived. On 4 August, Maurice and Maralyn took the fast train to Busan. As they went aboard the rusty ship, finally home, Maurice and Maralyn greeted their rescuers. They hung a garland of flowers around Suh's neck, and the three posed together for the cameras. Maurice and Suh wrapped their arms around each other like brothers. Maralyn stood just behind. They were transformed, Suh noticed. Flesh on their bones, eyes bright, their bodies able to hold themselves up. So *this* is what they looked like.

~

It was time to go. Ivor and Sally Davis, the journalists who'd interviewed them in Honolulu, invited them to stay at their beach house in Malibu, California. The Davises had grown fond of Maurice and Maralyn during the days they'd spent listening to their story. They offered to show them L.A., look after them. Why not? It put off going back to England.

Maurice and Maralyn waved goodbye to another crowd at Gimpo airport and boarded the plane. A crate they'd had specially made for the many gifts they'd been given would follow on a ship. Another ocean crossing and they landed at the airport in L.A. An official looked over their passports and pressed a stamp into each one: "U.S. Immigration Dept.: No Visa Required." Maurice was delighted. Celebrity had its advantages.

Off they went again, like windup toys. A special reception at the British consulate, visits to Disneyland and Universal Studios, a drive up to Corral Canyon and down Sunset Boulevard. In between, "they ate us out of house and home," Ivor recalled. "Just eating and eating and eating."

As they were returning from a trip to the Hollywood Bowl to hear the Boston Symphony Orchestra, a car drove into the back of Ivor's Volvo, damaging it badly. Everyone was fine, but Ivor panicked. Here were a pair who'd survived the open ocean, and he'd almost gotten them killed on the freeway.

One afternoon, Maurice decided to skip an outing and went to the beach by himself. For nearly two months, they'd been on show, performing their appreciative dance over and over again. It can be exhausting, being a guest.

Maurice sat and looked out to the ocean, the light glancing off the low waves. It was hard to believe that it was the same ocean on which they'd fished, struggled, lived. There was an innocence to the ordeal now. They hadn't known what it meant, or what it would become.

It felt wonderful, for a moment, to step away. Maurice realised that this was the first time in his life he'd sat still on a beach. "I have landed on them, walked on them, swam from them, even had snacks on them," he wrote, but he had never just sat on one and done nothing. Until now, sunbathing had been one of many human behaviours he'd found perplexing. Relaxation, to Maurice, was close to moral degradation. But here, now, alone for the first time in months, he simply sat. He didn't have to say nice things about what he was seeing. He didn't have to pose for a photograph. He didn't have to try to make himself understood.

He was still so *tired*, a tiredness that felt as if it had taken root somewhere deep and incurable in his body. Sitting on the sand, alone, he could rest. Solitude, when chosen, can feel like such a gift.

SIX

The white Pan Am jet descended into London through heavy cloud. They were such practised flyers now, crossing oceans back and forth. Ivor had bought their tickets, good old Ivor, and then bought new tickets on a different flight once they discovered their itinerary had been leaked to the press. After the onslaught in Honolulu and Seoul, they couldn't face another bank of reporters in an arrivals lounge.

Not long before they landed, Maurice wobbled along the aisle to wash in one of the cramped toilet cubicles, and a jolt of turbulence sent hot water flying out of the sink, soaking his trousers.

Why can flying into England feel so bleak? It wasn't just that he looked as if he'd wet himself. Below was a landscape they thought they'd never see again. Rows of back gardens, separated by fences; dark-windowed houses and boxy fields; thin lines of cars processing down grey roads. A view of England from above seems to promise a safe and orderly life, which might have been consoling to Maurice and Maralyn if that was not precisely the life they'd hoped to escape.

England was where they'd started, and where they would have to start again. The ex–Navy Commander Erroll Bruce, who ran the Nautical Publishing Company in Lymington, Hampshire, wanted to publish their account as quickly as possible, while the story was still fresh in the public's minds. A book, Maurice knew, would help to pay for the next voyage. Their future depended on the money they could make out of their past.

And the future, really, was all Maralyn wanted to think about. The new boat. The next trip. It was like a compulsion, according to friends: to only look forward.

But *England*. For weeks now they had been in constant motion. After Hawaii, South Korea, California, it was as if they were being lowered through the clouds into a trap. And what were they coming back to? No home to speak of, and a country that appeared to be unravelling. England, according to its press, was not only in temporary crisis due to the oil shock, inflation, and industrial strikes but in terminal decline. The threat of IRA bombing loomed. Ted Heath, the prime minister, was only a few months away from making a speech in which he'd announce the three-day week and warn the population that their Christmas would be dreadful. The country was spent, visibly spoiling, an idea gone bad.

A car, arranged by Erroll Bruce, drove them from the airport through clogged traffic into town. Wet from August rain, London had that dirty, worn-out look it gets in late summer.

They pulled up at the entrance of the Royal Lancaster hotel overlooking Hyde Park. The hotel, an austere tower block, had only opened in 1967. From the top floor you could see the Round Pond and a wash of plane trees.

Waiting for them outside was a camera crew from the BBC. Maralyn, sick of the attention, rushed past them into the lobby, refusing to speak.

Maurice, conscious of their press obligations, had to persuade her to come back and be interviewed, promising that once this one was done, they'd be left in peace, which was hardly likely given that ITN was already waiting for them inside.

In their room, Maralyn called June, the bosun. They hadn't spoken since their rescue, which Colin and June had happened to hear about on the radio while on holiday in Wales. They must come for dinner, come and stay at the hotel, said Maralyn. The Fosketts drove straight up to London.

In the hotel restaurant that evening, the four talked for so long that the food turned cold, the room emptied, and the headwaiter had to ask them to leave. Colin and June wanted to hear everything, the whole story, the sinking and survival, but Maurice and Maralyn kept moving the conversation on, as if it weren't interesting to go over it all again. All they wanted to talk about was the next voyage. Then came the offer. Once they'd built their new boat, would Colin and June like to come with them to Patagonia?

Perhaps it was the high spirits, the sentimentality of reunion, the sense of adventure narrowly survived and more in the offing, but with hardly a discussion between them the Fosketts said yes. It was only later that Colin realised what he'd agreed to, the scale and risk of the trip, the disruption it would cause to their lives. They'd have to give up their jobs. It would mean months at sea. Colin called his brother to tell him what he'd done. His brother replied, "You're absolutely mad."

~

The next morning, Maurice and Maralyn were driven by chauffeur to Lymington to stay in Erroll Bruce's white-gated mansion, where the gardens gave way to paddocks and the lane ended at the sea. They had their photograph taken strolling across the lawn hand in hand, both in checked shirts, Maurice with socks under his sandals, Maralyn in flares.

Lymington, close to where they'd begun, was unchanged. A contented, affluent market town with a pretty high street from which cobbled streets led down to a quay full of yachts. Locals could sail straight out from the two marinas into the Solent for their jaunts along the coast. Amateur sailors, brief excursions; nothing like what they'd done. "Maralyn and I could detect a curious enigma of having lived in two different worlds," Maurice reflected.

England seemed even worse than Maurice remembered. All the old structures, still standing, as if they mattered. A corrupt, chaotic political system. Adulation doled out to footballers and pop stars: George Best, David Bowie, beautiful men with startling hair who were worshipped like gods. A population obsessed by the *monarchy*, of all things.

Princess Anne and Mark Phillips had recently announced their engagement on the lawns of Buckingham Palace. Anne, in a pink suit and silk scarf, had shown off her ring on television: a single sapphire flanked by diamonds. The country was agog.

Maurice felt like a veteran from a long and distant war returning home to find people concerned with the minor preoccupations of their own lives and the wedding day of a princess. What would she *wear*? He'd known what it was to live at the edge of death.

Maralyn, meanwhile, was consumed by their plans. No one seemed to understand their desire to return to sea, and people often asked why they didn't buy a house instead. "If your house burnt down, you'd build another house," Maralyn would reply. "But my home had sunk, so I'm going to build another home."

All the continued media interest, however, "filled her with a sense of utmost annoyance," wrote Maurice. They had to play along, especially with those who might help to equip their next trip. Allied Polymer, the company that had made the fabric of the life raft, asked them to visit its factory by helicopter. They launched the Whitbread round-the-world yacht race in Portsmouth. The Avon Rubber Company, manufacturers of the dinghy and the life raft, invited them to open its new factory in Llanelli, South Wales. Maurice wore a suit, Maralyn her checked coat. They posed, grinning, in front of a map of the Pacific Ocean showing their route, the line turning from solid to dotted after the sinking of their boat. And then again, holding a Welsh flag next to a newly unveiled plaque:

THIS FACTORY WAS OPENED BY
MAURICE AND MARALYN BAILEY
TO COMMEMORATE THEIR 117 DAYS ADRIFT
IN THE PACIFIC OCEAN DURING 1973 IN
AN AVON LIFE RAFT AND DINGHY.

Even the dealer from whom they'd bought their first car asked them for publicity. Mostly, they said yes. Fame would sell the book, and they needed the cash. A lot of cash, to fund a voyage. The *Express*'s £10,000 would cover much of the boat's initial building costs, but not the whole trip and all their supplies. Compared with their peers, they were in a financially precarious position. While they'd been away at sea, getting poorer, their friends had been getting better jobs, buying bigger houses.

Still, Maurice refused to complain, at least out loud.

Think of what they'd gained. "We had found self-knowledge, self-reliance and proved our emotional self-sufficiency." As if it were an achievement, to need no one else.

~

There was, soon enough, a coming down to earth. Maurice wasn't well. At Southampton General Hospital, they discovered a cavity in his lung. The clot he'd coughed up on the raft had left a hole.

From the Bruces' mansion, they moved around, including a stint with Colin and June. That didn't last long. The garden gate squeaked. Colin found Maurice out there at all hours, oiling it. Eventually, they moved to a rented flat over the Tesco on Lymington High Street. No squeaking gate. It would do.

Bruce wanted to publish the following spring. Maurice didn't work well under pressure; he liked to write slowly and carefully, checking and rechecking his sources to ensure accuracy. And how do you write about such an experience? How do you reduce it to sentences? He had the logbook, his charts, records of observations and wind speeds, Maralyn's diary, but none of these captured the feeling of time slowing to the point of vacancy, the hours of emptiness, the blank space of the ocean.

Maurice could rely only on what he knew for certain, a litany of facts. He proceeded chronologically, unafraid of jargon. "I clipped the luff on the port lifeline whilst Maralyn made the sheet fast to starboard." There were few concessions to readers unfamiliar with the lexicon of sailing.

And yet, at the same time, writing the book allowed Maurice to reflect a little on how they'd survived. It was all Maralyn: her optimism, her faith. "She had that essential gift of leadership and showed by her own example the willpower needed to keep life going," he wrote. He wasn't afraid, either, of revealing his despair. There seemed no point in denying it when it was true.

Maralyn, meanwhile, wrote her own account, briefer than Maurice's. She drew on her diary, and offered mostly factual observation, with the occasional blast of frustration. Often, she simply explained one of her innovations, like the playing cards, which measured approximately two inches by three inches, or her safety-pin fishhooks, which got them "back in the fishing business." Even now, she couldn't help sounding gung ho.

Their passages alternated, each one printed with the name of its author. Some were marked with a subtitle: "The Fifteenth Turtle"; "Maurice Makes a Bonfire"; "We Talk of Death." At times, the tone was so matter-of-fact that it read like a dual account of an unremarkable holiday that took a slightly unconventional turn.

To fill it all out, they included maps, Maralyn's pictures of the boat sinking, and grainy photographs of her diary. It was like a collection of evidence from a crime scene, as if to prove it had all really happened. A series of illustrations depicted all the birds and fish they saw, and some of their escapades on the raft.

One of the larger drawings was of the giant wave. Maurice is shown falling backwards out of the dinghy, bottom in the ocean. Maralyn looks down at him from the opening in the raft, one arm delicately extended to its edge, as if she were leaning out of an upstairs window to call him in for tea.

~

The book, *117 Days Adrift*, was published in April 1974. On the cover of its first edition was a colour photograph of Maurice bent over in the dinghy, clinging to the rope thrown from the *Wolmi*. The raft is to the left, a white-tipped swell beneath both vessels. Maralyn is nowhere to be seen.

A publisher's note, whose specificity has strong echoes of Maurice, was included at the start, explaining over five paragraphs that the title of the book was inaccurate and that they had in fact survived on the life raft for 118 and one-third days. They had stuck with the error for the title, because "the adventure was generally known as such from the initial news reports." You don't abandon a piece of good branding.

A launch party was held in London, then another in Paris. They were so surrounded by guests at these events that, to Maurice's disappointment, they didn't have a chance to sample the food.

The day after the London launch, they toured the television studios, life raft in tow. In one interview, Maurice, in a suit, was made to change into a cameraman's woolly jumper in order to more closely resemble everyone's imagined idea of a sailor. At Harrods, the life raft was inflated for a display, then deflated and reinflated again at Selfridges. Then a tour: Southampton, Portsmouth, Bristol, Cardiff, Birmingham, Derby, Nottingham, Norwich, Sheffield, Manchester, Edinburgh, Glasgow. Interviews, talks, and photo shoots everywhere they went. "Will we ever eat or sleep?" wrote Maralyn in her diary. For *The Observer*, they were asked to hop in and out of the life raft and dinghy despite Maurice being in agony from a cracked rib where he'd slipped in the bath the night before.

At the Southampton Boat Show, they were jointly made Yachtsman of the Year. Maralyn went to the Savoy hotel to receive a Woman of the Year accolade. While the other guests stepped out of Jaguars and Daimlers, Maurice and June dropped her off in a Mini Traveller. At lunch, she sat opposite Margaret Thatcher, then education secretary, while Maurice and June went to eat at a Wimpy off Trafalgar Square.

At the London Boat Show at Earl's Court, they were in the middle of being photographed rowing in a dinghy, life jackets on over Maurice's smart suit and Maralyn's checked coat, when an IRA bomb threat was announced. The bomb, a small one, went off minutes after they left the hall, covering them with dust.

~

Most fame is odd and unreliable, but theirs—born of an accident—seemed especially precarious. It involved so much re-enactment, as if people could only believe what had happened to them if they saw a mocked-up version of it with their own eyes: Maurice and Maralyn mugging for cameras and grinning from dinghies. The raft, carted around from studio to photo shoot, was their proof.

As they did the circuit of studios, they found themselves meeting other famous people. They couldn't help it; once you're caught in that ecosystem, they're everywhere. After a BBC programme in Aberdeen, the Hollywood actress Patricia Neal, married to Roald Dahl, invited them to dinner. The naturalist Sir Peter Scott drove them round his wildlife park at Slimbridge, Gloucestershire—an honour that had previously been granted only to the queen and Prince Philip. Maurice was delighted.

Then, an American tour. New York, Cleveland, Philadelphia, Baltimore, Cincinnati, Boston. Their days started at 6:30 a.m., a car picking them up from their hotel and driving them straight to a studio.

Maralyn appeared on a popular game show, *To Tell the Truth.* A panel, the men in suits and the women in long gowns and pearls, had to pick from three contenders all claiming to be the central character of a true story that was told at the start. The world's strongest man; an illustrious stamp collector; a woman who had survived 118 and one-third days on a life raft.

Maralyn was the ideal guest: a face not famous enough to ruin the premise but with a story that made lively material for the host's introduction. Each contender stepped forward to state their identity: My name is Maralyn Bailey, my name is Maralyn Bailey, my name is Maralyn Bailey. The panel questioned them, trying to work out which was the real one. Who could most convincingly claim to have eaten turtles; who looked most likely to have half starved on a raft? The line between promotion and humiliation can be so fine. Filming a show at SeaWorld in Florida, they had to feign delight as dolphins and orcas were made to perform jumps. Surely anyone could see that the poor creatures were miserable, trapped in a game for the cameras, when they should be free, out at sea, where they belonged.

~

In New York, a publisher got in touch: Would they like to write the sequel to *117 Days Adrift*, an account of their next trip, to Patagonia? It was perfect. A new book would give their voyage urgency and purpose, and would mean more money. They enlisted the help of George Greenfield, a grand London literary agent, who represented Ranulph Fiennes and Stirling Moss.

Greenfield, who joked about accidentally exposing himself to Margaret Thatcher when his trouser zip fell down as he helped her sign Japanese contracts for her memoir, was frank. He wasn't sure that a voyage to Patagonia was exciting enough to sell.

They needed, Greenfield added, a clear goal for the journey in order to win the support of commercial sponsors and get coverage from the press.

Maurice and Maralyn weren't discouraged. The idea for the trip had come when they were adrift in the ocean: It had kept them alive. Patagonia was one of the last remaining wild places on Earth. They were following Darwin! Surely this was a worthy subject for a book.

Maurice wasn't quite able to grasp that it wasn't the voyage itself that had made their last book an attractive commercial proposition, but its failure. No one would have suggested they write a book of their travels if they'd arrived safely in New Zealand. No one wants to read the story of an adventure going *right.*

~

The publishers wanted a manuscript by July 1976. The journey would take at least nine months. To deliver on time, Maurice and Maralyn calculated that they'd have to leave England in July 1975. To be thoroughly tested, the boat would need to be ready in April.

She was being built at a yard in Teignmouth, Devon. Ever since they'd drawn her on the life raft, they'd known what they wanted: a forty-five-foot vessel, with a ketch rig, a good beam, a long straight keel, a draught of no more than six feet, and, for obvious reasons, a strong hull.

The costs were enormous and rising due to inflation. The rivets and fastenings alone came to £2,500. The "spiteful and illogical government," wrote Maurice, had added 25 per cent

VAT to boats and marine equipment, as if it had specifically had Maurice's project in mind.

Maralyn wrote to companies whose products they'd used on the last voyage, asking for anything they might be able to donate or sell to them at a discounted rate, in return for publicity. Greenfield secured an offer of food and clothes from Marks and Spencer. Avon, which had made their life raft and dinghy, agreed to act as a sponsor and underwrite some of the boat's costs.

Soon they'd be receiving royalties from *117 Days Adrift*. But in the meantime, they needed to live as cheaply as possible. Erroll Bruce suggested the Channel Islands: useful for tax. A friend of his owned a tiny cottage on the island of Alderney, which they could rent. Maurice and Maralyn knew the island from sailing across the Channel. They set up a limited company in Jersey and banked in Guernsey, like millionaires.

With everything they owned in the world packed into three suitcases, they boarded a tiny aeroplane and flew to Alderney. From the plane window, they could see the whole island, one half lined with high cliffs, the other with golden beaches and bays. Their cottage was on the edge of the town of St. Anne, at the end of a cobbled street: a tiny, whitewashed two-up, two-down with two-foot-thick stone walls and red chimney pots. Maurice liked to use the cottage's French address: 15 Petite Rue, Île d'Aurigny, Îles des Normandes.

Apart from attempts at organised fun with the island's expat community, people Maurice disliked for their snobbery and croquet, they were alone again on Alderney. It was a place marked by German occupation, with concrete fortifications and bunkers hidden beneath houses. Detached from the mainland, as Maurice took to calling it, the island allowed a kind of peace to return. Every day they walked a little farther than the last, building up their strength.

At night, as the wind howled, the cottage's roof slates shifted and rain leaked into their bedroom, where they slept on two single beds. The water always seemed to fall on Maralyn, however the beds were arranged. Maurice lay awake listening to her muttering as she pulled her bed around the room to avoid the drips.

When the lease expired on the cottage, they moved into an unfurnished brick bungalow, a place so overgrown with brambles that they had to borrow secateurs from a neighbour to cut a path to the front door. There were no beds, and no electricity, so they cooked on a Primus stove, had a Tilley paraffin lamp for light, and slept on the concrete floor. The comfort of discomfort. It was like being on a boat.

~

On the morning of 4 June 1975, their new boat was finally ready to be sailed. *Auralyn II* was dolled up like a show pony, bunting flying from her rigging. Avon had sent out invitations to a ceremony, inviting press, TV, local dignitaries. They would sail first to Lymington for their final preparations, then in stages to Llanelli and the Avon factory. From there, they'd start the voyage to Patagonia.

As the tide came in, a crowd began to form. Maurice and Maralyn, like their boat, were dressed up for the occasion, Maralyn in a jacket and wide-legged trousers, Maurice in a suit. The champagne bottle was suspended, waiting to be smashed against the side of the boat for the cameras.

Maralyn stepped forward in her smart black shoes. "I name this yacht *Auralyn* the Second!" she shouted, and released the bottle, which swung towards the bow, missed, struck the hull, and didn't break. She tried again, missed again. After the third failed attempt, momentum leaking fast, the boat's designer retrieved the bottle and instructed Maralyn to thwack it against the foot of the metal bobstay. Twice she tried, and nothing. Finally, on the sixth attempt, it smashed, Maralyn and Maurice laughed, the crowds cheered, and the winch was wound to draw the cable through the pulleys to haul the boat into the water. The boat didn't move. Volunteers emerged from the crowd and started to push *Auralyn* along the slipway as if she were an old banger stuck in the mud.

It wasn't quite how Maurice and Maralyn had pictured the first outing of their new vessel; all this undignified shoving. Eventually, she was eased down the slipway until her rudder entered the water, at which point she stopped and slid off the side, bending her steel cradle in the process. No one could move her an inch after that, and the tide began to go out. The builder actually cried. "The day," wrote Maurice, as if the unfolding calamity confirmed some deeper truth, "turned out to be a fiasco after all."

~

The slipway was repaired, the boat fixed. A few days later, they sailed to Lymington and a BBC presenter, Cliff Michelmore, came down to film with them for an episode of his travel show, *Globetrotter.*

Michelmore, dressed for the assignment in a red shirt beneath a cream cable-knit sweater, arrived on a bright, blowy day. The Solent was fretting in the wind. He interviewed them sitting on the roof of the cabin. Maralyn, in lilac trousers, had her legs tucked beneath her. Maurice swung his over the side, like a little boy who'd rather be playing. The wind kept blowing his wispy hair straight up from his head.

Michelmore seemed more interested in their last voyage than their next. He wanted a full account of that first hour, once they knew she was going to sink. Maralyn spoke first, so practised at telling the story that she smiled gamely as she described pumping out the water and stuffing the hole with cushions.

Surely Maurice was anxious about Maralyn not being able to swim, said Michelmore. "Well, yes, this was always a worrying feature," said Maurice, in his high, precise voice, each word enunciated as if to stop it from escaping in the wind. They both looked delighted, as though it were all an amusement now. Maralyn said she'd have found a way, if she'd had to.

What about the turtles, how did they know which parts to eat? Once you'd cut the thing open, said Maralyn, it was like any animal and easy to spot the kidneys, liver, intestines, and so on. "It doesn't take long to find your way around."

Did they ever try to eat a bird? Michelmore, it seemed, had not read the book. Maurice patiently explained that they'd caught eight. It had all become almost ordinary to them, told so many times that Maurice had developed a structure: the first phase, when they rowed; the second phase, when they were blown north by the wind; and the third phase, when they were carried west, far out into the ocean. "It was in that third phase," said Maurice, "that our morale began to ebb," as if his morale had been perfectly intact until then.

Michelmore kept on. How had they passed all that formless time? "We found always a need to plan for the future," said Maralyn. "This planning for the future helped to keep us sane, I'm sure." Or at least it kept her sane enough to keep Maurice sane, or thereabouts.

Almost as an afterthought, Michelmore asked about the new boat. Was it really the same as the one they had planned while adrift? Maralyn smiled: "She's very close, I'm sure." Maurice smiled too, with a kind of tense pride: "She conforms *exactly* to the ideas we formulated in that life raft."

When Michelmore asked what the difference was between this boat and the last, Maurice listed various small adjustments: greater quantities of food, more carbohydrates than protein, a stainless-steel knife for filleting fish. And one key addition: rocket flares.

~

They sailed for Llanelli via Falmouth, past Lizard Point, where the land falls down into the sea in rocky slopes and sandy coves edge the clear water. A basking shark swam alongside the boat around the tip of the peninsula, as if acting as a guide.

At St. Ives, its rows of pretty windows facing out to sea, they went ashore. *Globetrotter* was about to air, and they didn't want to miss it. Running through the old lanes of the town, Maralyn found a man up a ladder painting his house and asked if they could come in. He made them tea, and they sat on his sofa to watch themselves on television.

It was a jaunty show, *Globetrotter*, with its opening montage of speedboats, spiders, and aeroplanes accompanied by a swing band soundtrack. "July 1973," said Michelmore in a mode of high drama, "Maurice and Maralyn made the headlines in all our morning papers."

There were all the morning papers, fanned out to reveal the headlines: BRITONS SAVED AFTER 117 DAYS ON RAFT; SHIPWRECKED COUPLE CAUGHT SHARKS ON SAFETY PINS; ATTACK BY AN ANGRY WHALE BEGAN COUPLE'S 117-DAY ORDEAL; 117 DAYS OF HELL.

Michelmore was perched on the side of the life raft in a jacket and tie. How many times had the knackered craft now been wheeled out? Harrods, Selfridges, boat shows, photo shoots, now here, in a BBC studio. Holding a silver pointer, Michelmore showed where Maralyn had carefully etched the passing days on its side, "MY BIRTHDAY" clearly visible. Then a picture of Maurice's logbook:

> *Holed below waterline. All efforts to save ship failed. Abandoned ship. Took to life raft. Situation desperate and bleak. Completed 7269 miles since leaving England, 256 days, 177 engine hours.*

A crisis privately contained by numbers in a book, now on television for all to see. Then pictures of their inventions: the safety-pin hook; Maralyn's fish catcher; and, at last, the stars themselves on the deck of *Auralyn II*, tearing across the sea in matching orange raincoats. "I went down to Lymington to talk to them about their new voyage, and their last one," explained Michelmore, before the interview in which he asked them almost exclusively about the last one.

In the final shot, Maurice tightened a knot, and that was it, their story was over, reduced to a segment about ten minutes long.

~

The crew assembled. Tony, an old school friend of Maralyn's from Derby, joined in Devon; Colin and June in Llanelli. Tony's wife had recently died, and Maralyn thought the distraction of the trip might be good for him. They'd all given up jobs to come aboard and weren't being paid but had agreed, according to Maurice, that "the experience would be compensation enough."

Maurice assigned everyone their duties. He remained skipper, navigator, and "chronicler"; Maralyn was the galley manager; June, the bosun, was put in charge of the upkeep of the sails, cordage, and dinghies; Colin was the ship's carpenter; Tony, the engineer.

They got to work, mending deck leaks, overhauling electrics, setting up the rigging and treating it with linseed oil. With the help of workers from the Avon factory, overseen by Maralyn, they stocked the galley with nearly two thousand tins, jars, and packets of food, most of it given by Marks and Spencer. Boots donated all their medical supplies—enough, noted Maurice, for them to be able to perform minor surgery on board.

It was different, having a crew. Sailing round the wild and rocky islands of Patagonia would be treacherous, the extra hands were essential, but Maurice knew that the presence of others made the expedition less romantic than their last. "Certainly," he wrote, "if we were thinking of the media—and the reaction to our recent ordeal had taught us to think that way—we knew the voyage would be better undertaken by ourselves."

That was the picture everyone wanted. The two of them alone, waving from the deck, as they sailed towards whales and storms and possible death, all the unknowable events of a long voyage. Fame had taught Maurice one of its many questionable lessons: that it is possible to perform life for the sake of a good photograph.

Days to go, and a gale was forecast. A ceremony had been organised, and the press was already invited. They couldn't change the date. The conditions couldn't have been worse. The captains of the pilot boats who would guide them out of the harbour suggested that they set off as planned, then anchor for the night off Burry Port, five miles away. They could wait there until the weather calmed down. It would be a fake departure for the cameras, but that didn't matter. They'd say goodbye, sail away, then hide out of sight.

The morning of 15 July was grey and gusty, rain threatening

from a bank of low clouds. "A day when wise sailors stayed in harbour," noted Maurice. The people of Llanelli gathered to see them off. The mayor bade them farewell. A local vicar gave them a package of Welsh-language hymnbooks to give to the Welsh community in Patagonia. "We all made speeches," wrote Maurice.

The dock was lined with smiling, expectant faces, hands raised and waving. Beyond, the open water waited for them, rough and white. As the dock gates opened, the crowd cheered. Maurice cast off the lines, and they motored out into the storm. It was a glorious farewell, all for show.

Part Four

A theatrical departure in front of a well-wishing crowd followed by a long voyage on which you might be shipwrecked: It's not bad, as metaphors go, for the relationship between a wedding and a marriage.

The flowers have been arranged; the lockers stocked. There's a new dress; a new boat. The couple kiss outside a registry office; wave from a deck.

Beneath the performance lies a sense of ending. It's not just the departure—newlyweds driving away in a car; the boat cutting through the water until it disappears from view. Something irrevocable is taking place in the spirit of hope.

In that sense, it's a beginning too. A new chapter, as people like to say, giving credence to the falsehood that our lives unfold like stories. There's such trust in that moment. Trust in what is to come; trust in how well it will all go.

And then what? After the wedding, after the honeymoon—well, then it's just *days*. Ordinary days. The insurmountable, self-renewing chores. The bins, the laundry, the procession of meals. And those are the golden days, it turns out. The blissful, boring days that you long for when things go wrong. It's not as if we weren't warned. The old vows knew what they were doing: for better, for worse; for richer, for poorer; in sickness and in health. The storms are right there in the words.

Misfortune can seem abstract in the midst of celebration. At the beginning, we imagine the bad weather might pass us by. It's only natural, part of the long business of self-preservation, because how impossible it would be to go through life in full awareness of all that will befall us.

Somewhere, deep within, unspoken, we must know, we *do* know, that we'll all have our time adrift. For what else is a marriage, really, if not being stuck on a small raft with someone and trying to survive?

~

Years later, Maralyn told interviewers that their survival had been a team effort. On the raft, she and Maurice worked in partnership, each supporting the other equally. "Where one faltered, the other bolstered their flagging spirits," she said to a dumbfounded John Peel, who found it hard to believe that having been adrift on an ocean for four months, they'd decided to go sailing again.

Maurice was always more candid. In his version, he'd done all the flagging and she'd done all the bolstering. Had he been alone on the ocean, he would have given up. Death would have come disguised as relief. Or, if it was taking too long, he'd have swum away from the raft and drowned.

Perhaps it was modesty that stopped Maralyn from being honest about how things had actually been: the extent to which she'd had to prop Maurice up or navigate his moods. Or perhaps it was an instinctive protectiveness. It would have felt cruel, maybe, to paint a true picture of his struggle.

Once, an interviewer asked Maralyn how Maurice had helped *her*. "I think it was having someone else to think about, rather than think about myself all the time," she replied. "It was thinking about him and helping him." His need had been her occupation. Without her, what would have become of him?

Part Five

ONE

Every Sunday, at about half past nine in the morning, Maurice went to sit at table 17 in the corner of the Tea House in Lyndhurst, a small town near the south coast of England. The café had dark green signs and large picture windows, and stood on a corner of the high street. It served steak and ale pies for lunch and fresh scones with jam and clotted cream for tea. At the counter, behind glass fronts, were displays of homemade cakes, thickly iced.

Hilary, the owner, was fond of Maurice. The week was patterned by people like him, regulars coming in for their favourite meal on their particular day. Maurice was so consistent that she'd know something was wrong if he didn't walk through the door shortly after opening on a Sunday.

"How are you today, Mr. Bailey?" she always asked. "Not very good," Maurice would reply.

Hilary reserved his table. If it wasn't available, he wouldn't come in. It was table 17 or nothing. He'd order a tea cake or a cheese scone, and coffee, which Hilary brought over in a cafetière. When she'd taken over the teahouse, there weren't any cafetières, but Maurice let it be known that this was how he liked his coffee, with cream on the side, so she bought one especially for him.

Then Maurice read his book. Jean and Dave usually came in at about this time, the other Sunday morning regulars. Jean would go over to Maurice's table and say hello, but he tended not to ask her to sit down. She didn't mind. Usually they'd have a chat, and he might tell her a story from his travels. Just five or ten minutes, not more. Then he went back to reading.

Maurice had become old. The hunch in his back had worsened over time, tilting his head to one side so that he often looked as if he were peering up at things. The little that was left of his hair had turned stark white, growing in low tufts above his ears. He was entirely deaf in one ear and halfway there in the other. He always looked smart, though, in formal trousers and a jumper or jacket, and a shirt that had evidently been ironed.

Before he left the teahouse, he pocketed a cream paper napkin from the table to take home and stash in a drawer with all the other cream paper napkins he had taken on previous Sundays.

Once, when he was paying his bill at the till, Hilary asked what he was going to do that day. Maurice replied, "Oh, maybe go and jump in front of those cars outside."

In fact, there was bell-ringing to get to. Back in the car, Maurice drove to wherever the bells needed to be rung for the Sunday service: either up the high street at St. Michaels and All

Angels, whose wooden, winged angels are lodged in the roof, or at St. Mary's, Eling, with its large yew and tilting gravestones, names fading from the weather and time, or at All Saints, Minstead, where the church resembles a cottage from a fairy tale, buried deep in the forest. At the foot of the bell tower is a white wooden door. It is difficult not to imagine a winding staircase behind it, a girl imprisoned at the top. Not long after Maralyn died, Maurice made a donation towards the purchase of one of the bells in her memory.

Bells rung, sermon delivered, parishioners blessed, Maurice would return home to his bungalow on Greenmead Avenue in Everton, a village on the edge of Lymington. The bungalow was called Lynaura, another way of melding their names. Hers first, this time.

At the back was a two-hundred-foot garden with two sheds, a garage and a greenhouse, a vegetable patch and a long lawn. Maurice's old mower wasn't up to the job, so his neighbour Jamie often came round to do it for him. On cooler days, the sea winds blew in and unsettled the leaves of two silver birches, some apple trees, and a willow. Maurice couldn't eat the apples; he suffered from diverticulitis and they upset his stomach. Clumps of daffodils interrupted the lawn with yellow in the spring. A small pond contained a koi carp, the Japanese variety, bright orange and white. Colin and June would already be there, waiting for him. They had their own key. Something vegetarian that June had prepared at home and brought over in a covered dish on her lap in the car would be cooking in the oven. Neither he nor Maralyn had eaten meat since all those turtles on the life raft, apart from some tins on the Patagonia voyage.

Maurice had rules for June's cooking. No mushrooms or onions; he didn't like those. June sometimes found it hard to think of vegetarian dishes that *didn't* contain mushrooms or onions, but she tried. By the time Maurice opened the front door, the meal would be three-quarters cooked: He liked it to be nearly but not quite ready when he got home.

"How are you today?" June would ask. "Suicidal again," he'd reply.

TWO

Sometimes, when Sunday rolled around again, Colin told June to go and visit Maurice on her own. He couldn't face it. He worked six days a week as a carpenter for a building firm, and Sunday was his only day off. Visiting Maurice didn't always feel like a day off.

As soon as Colin walked through the door, Maurice presented him with a list of jobs. House jobs, garden jobs, anything that needed fixing. Colin did his best, but he tried to avoid the trickier ones, the tasks that required drilling or hours of manual labour. I haven't got my tools, he'd say. It being a Sunday and my only day off, he didn't say. Maurice replied, "There are tools in the shed."

Once, Maurice asked Colin to repair a window in his greenhouse. It was a fiddly job: replacing the glass, getting it to fit. The greenhouse was in a state anyway, so Colin told him to get a new one. "Oh," said Maurice. He went quiet for a while, then said to Colin, "Are you *sure* you don't want to work on that greenhouse?" He kept asking all afternoon, the way a child will continually ask for a biscuit once the possibility of a biscuit has been mentioned. Colin went to have a look.

With June, Maurice would wordlessly hand her a jumper, and she'd take it home and mend it. Sometimes she'd come back from these Sundays exhausted, having been teased and needled by him all day.

It had been the same on the Patagonia trip, those fourteen long months on *Auralyn II*. June, usually resilient, had gradually been reduced to fragments by Maurice. In charge of keeping the rigging and sails in good order, she was always mending, but whatever she did, however she did it, he noticed errors, pointed them out, and picked at her, knowing that she couldn't, or wouldn't, defend herself. Often, she'd end up in tears, being comforted by Maralyn.

Colin said it was like watching a cat with a mouse, the way it would flick its prey between its claws, not always to kill, but for sport. Maurice was a tyrant on that trip. He told his crew that on the boat he was God, which was funny given that he'd never believed in the idea. But that was how he said it, I am God. A benevolent God, but more Greek than Christian; a dispenser of judgement, rather than forgiveness.

Maybe it was having a crew that made him despotic. Last time, he and Maralyn had done it all themselves and had established the way things should be done, or at least the way they liked things to be done. Now there were other people with their own ideas, and different methods. Colin, June, and Tony didn't stand a chance: He held them to standards that were by definition impossible to meet because they were the standards he set for himself. Maurice rarely approved of himself, so it was unlikely he'd see anything but imperfection in others.

To everyone's relief, Maralyn, the Holy Spirit, quietly maintained her authority on the boat. Maurice usually deferred to her on all matters, apart from when he didn't. Maralyn, for example, wanted to peel the potatoes before cooking them. Maurice thought peeling was a ridiculous waste of time. Neither would give way. Ping-pong, ping-pong. A muted, terse sort of argument, the kind whose energy intensifies the more you try to contain it. Neither seemed willing to shout at the other, and neither was inclined to surrender. Perhaps that's why their arguments, though rare, lasted so long. After the potatoes, there was a day, even two, of tight silence until Maurice backed down.

Everyone on that boat, apart from Maralyn, had taken enough money with them to buy a flight home from the farthest point of the voyage. An emergency fund, in case they were unwell or simply couldn't bear another day at sea, of damp and exhaustion and gruelling work. No one had said, in case they couldn't bear another day of Maurice. Once, in the Gulf of Mexico, Maurice fell over while on deck, and Colin and June found themselves imagining chucking him overboard.

After one upset, June implored Colin to let them leave, get on a plane, go home. But Colin had promised himself to see it through to the end and he persuaded her to stay.

It was harder for Maralyn's friend Tony. Maurice, knowing that he'd have to spend much of the trip shut away in his cabin writing the second book, had appointed Tony the substitute skipper. Though he'd made the arrangement himself, Maurice found it almost intolerable. He kept rising up from the cabin and overriding Tony's instructions, taking control despite himself. Tony became miserable, fed up with being undermined and irritated by the way Maurice spoke to him and to Colin and June, too, as if they were skivvies.

Halfway across the Atlantic, Colin sensed a shift in the air. The atmosphere of a small boat is legible like that: Other people's passing moods are as unavoidable as the weather. One evening, Tony went to sleep in one frame of mind, resigned and bleak, and emerged in another. Demob happy, perhaps, except it was more relief than happiness. He'd decided to quit. Once they docked at Montevideo, on the south coast of Uruguay, Tony helped to refit and repair the boat, then got off and flew home.

"It gradually became apparent that he did not possess that ingrained ability to suffer the numerous small hardships and irksome duties that brands a real seaman," Maurice wrote later. Hiscock still loomed. Tony lacked seamanship, the greatest crime.

The problem now, thought Colin, decades after the voyage to Patagonia, was that without Maralyn there was no one to temper Maurice. No one to translate him or smooth his edges. Maurice was hard work. He liked to trip you up, to poke fun, to use words you wouldn't understand. He was absurdly particular about everything. However much you felt for the man, so obviously adrift in the world, severed by loneliness, it was sometimes hard to like him.

THREE

By the spring of 2002, treatment for cancer had swollen Maralyn's face and body so much that she no longer looked like herself. In late April, she and Maurice went on holiday to the Lake District with their dog Beda, a huge Rhodesian Ridgeback, and celebrated her sixty-first birthday with a candlelit dinner in the wooden cabin where they were staying. There was no more camping in the orange tent now. A short row of birthday cards and a vase of red and white roses decorated the table. Maralyn raised a glass as Maurice took a photograph, though either the swelling or her mood did not permit her to smile.

Her last walk, a stick in each hand, was on a day so grey that the landscape appeared colourless, drained of light. Slowly, they made their way along the level path around Tarn Hows, a glassy pool of still water encircled by conifers. It was a short and gentle walk, only a mile and a half, manageable for someone so unwell.

She died less than a month later, on 21 May 2002, while they were away again, staying in a cottage in Withypool, Somerset. She'd wanted one last voyage.

Before he came home, Maurice had her body cremated in Taunton. He took a picture of the crematorium, a squat modern building with privet hedges outside, and another of her wooden coffin, gold handles along the side, lying on a slab of dark marble. Later, he put these pictures in a large blue album he made to document her life. Beneath each image, he stuck carefully typed captions:

TAUNTON CREMATORIUM.

The coffin just before cremation. 24 May 2002.

Once home, he took her ashes to the New Forest. In the presence of Colin, June, Maralyn's half sister, Pat, and various other friends, he scattered her at the Naked Man, the remains of an old oak tree that had been used to hang highwaymen and smugglers. The tree now stands gnarly and alone, enclosed by a fence on a flat expanse of open heathland at the edge of the forest. Ponies graze nearby. Yellow gorse sprouts from the earth.

It has always meant something to people, this place. There are remains of a wreath against the trunk; a toy hangs from a branch. Maurice and Maralyn used to walk here with Beda, down the long path from the car park, past the tree, round in a loop, crossing the plain. On an overcast day, the boggy heath seems to blend into the sky, the horizon imperceptible. It is a little like being at sea.

~

5 June, 2002

Dear Marion and Denis,

I write to thank you most sincerely for your kind condolences at this agonizing time. Your words bring succour to the deep and permanent hurt I bear as a result of Maralyn's death. She died, as she had wanted, while we were away on what was to prove our last holiday together.

Maralyn and I were united in mutual support and we wove a fabric of love to wrap around the sinister threat of her impending demise. Over the last few weeks it sustained us, giving us some faith in the value of life.

Maralyn had a courage which was not easy to come by but which always endured. Her will was like the thrust of life itself—inexhaustible and as stubborn as the upsurge of Spring.

I think I will grieve for a long time to come (parting is such hell), but sooner or later I will strive to be the self Maralyn had known. For the moment, though, I am possessed of a fear derived from a paralysis of lonely despair, of uncertainty, of helplessness, of a knowledge that each nuance of feeling will adversely affect my confidence to cope with anything and everything.

But I can keep in my heart all the treasured memories of nearly forty years of life with Maralyn. Nothing can now deface that and it will become a gratifying base for future happiness.

Once again my grateful thanks. With all my best wishes.

Yours ever Maurice

In any sensible universe, he would have died first.

If it had been only grief, only loneliness, things might have been manageable. Both states are to be expected after the loss of a partner; both could be addressed. But Maurice's mind, without Maralyn's to keep it in line, veered into other territory.

In December 2003, a year and a half after Maralyn's death, he wrote a letter to a friend, B.

> *I wince whenever I think what little I did for her in those months—never for one moment believing she was to die until it was too late. Even now I cannot make peace with that. In analysis I think I must have been frightened, taking too much for granted, not caring to listen to any consideration suggesting a dire prognosis. I am haunted with guilt. . . . {I}t has taken time for me to grasp the depth of my neglect and thoughtlessness. Affecting everything is my remorse at this failure so that I am continuously troubled by disconsolate thoughts.*

Maurice knew what his mind was doing. He'd turned grief into punishment. There was no reason to persecute himself, especially now, but then he'd never needed a reason. Depression sets the cleverest traps. Maurice's thoughts sounded logical, one appeared to lead to the next, but really, they circled. He felt he had failed and could not correct his mistake, which heightened his sense of failure. Everywhere he turned, he found himself pointing out his errors. Round and round and round.

For forty years, Maurice had depended on Maralyn to untangle him. Now he was stuck. He talked of killing himself so often that his doctor arranged to see him once a month. Suicide was only ever an idea, a thought. But like all his thoughts, the more he thought it, the easier it was to think it again. The thought recurred; it dug a path.

Maurice's GP was a kind and patient woman. He liked talking to her. She was knowledgeable and pragmatic; someone who seemed to know what to do and how to do things, just as Maralyn had been. She happened to be a friend of his neighbour Jamie, and in conversations over the fence Maurice would hint at his admiration for this GP, half joking. Jamie would remind him—also joking, but with a certain emphasis—that she was married with two children. It's not going to happen, Maurice.

Still, Maurice discovered where she lived and took to driving past her house occasionally, not to say or do anything. Maurice was an awkward man with delicate manners in considerable pain. There was no possibility of threat. He just wanted to be somewhere in her orbit, close to her fortitude, as if he'd sensed that she was a sturdy kind of person, capable of holding him up.

FOUR

There are questions for the widowed. Such as what now? What shape will your life take? What, or who, will fill the emptiness? Can you learn to live alongside the emptiness, or will the emptiness swallow you whole?

It was quite obvious to anyone who knew Maurice that without Maralyn he did not know how to live. This was not a clichéd summation of his grief. He did not know *how* to live. He did not know what the days were for. She had always known for them both.

Before she died, knowing the extent to which Maurice would be unable to cope, Maralyn had tried to organise his future. Only Maralyn would think she had the power to plan other people's lives beyond the limits of her own existence. But Maurice needed taking care of. She had someone in mind: their friend B., who lived nearby.

Maurice was not averse to the idea of B. He liked her, she

had been close to Maralyn, and she didn't seem to mind him. He asked Colin round to redecorate the second bedroom in the bungalow for her. Colin painted the walls and overhauled the wardrobes. Maurice bought new bed linen and coat hangers.

But B., it turned out, did not want to look after Maurice. She stayed where she was, then moved to Wales. Maralyn hadn't planned for that.

For a while, he still had Beda. How Maralyn had loved that dog, throwing him birthday parties and making him cakes. But not long after Maralyn died, Beda fell ill and had to be put down. Maurice, bereft again, scattered the dog's ashes at the Naked Man, too.

About two weeks after *that*, Maurice went out into his garden and discovered that the koi carp had somehow leapt out of the pond, landed on the ground, and died. He went straight round to tell Jamie, as if such targeted misfortune, such clear evidence that the world was working against him, were so unbelievable that it required a witness.

~

There was the problem of time and what to do with it. Maurice tried to use it up. At home, he maintained standards. He wasn't one of those widowers who stopped washing in the absence of a wife. An ironing board was almost always erected downstairs for his shirts.

The kitchen was red tiled and pine, and narrow, like a galley. In the living room, books lined the walls and lay open on a reading table with Maurice's handwritten notes beside them. Logs were arranged in two wood-burning stoves. Maralyn had laid the fires not long before she died. Maurice, believing them to be the last things she'd touched in the house, decided they would never be lit.

Much of his time he spent in his study, a grand term for the box room between the two bedrooms, where he wrote letters on his typewriter, or his old word processor, a hefty, wayward machine that was constantly failing him. Eventually, under Jamie's patient guidance, he replaced it with a laptop.

This took some doing. Maurice did not like the new versions of things. He took issue with modern fonts, for example, claiming from his long experience in printing presses that the point sizes on the computer were wrong. He resisted switching to metric measurements, and refused to use the newer crosshead screws, keeping a supply of old, single-slotted screws in his shed.

It was how he'd sailed: clinging to the old ways, as if by being old, they were implicitly superior. Anything modern implied decline, further proof of the way things were going, which was badly. It was a strange logic, as if by measuring things in miles and ounces, you could not only arrest the passing of time but retain a kind of moral purity. Maurice's attitude seemed only to build a wall around him, with everything on the other side judged to be bad. It is lonely, being self-righteous.

~

He tried to see people, tried to talk. There were the regular fixtures. Sunday mornings in the teahouse with Hilary, Dave, and Jean. Sunday lunches with Colin and June. A fortnightly meal with a friend from Bournemouth, doctor's appointments, over-the-fence chats with Jamie, visits from his cleaner, who sat and talked more than she cleaned, surely knowing it was the more essential service. But it was bell-ringing, with all its practices and services, that filled his week.

There had been no spiritual epiphany. Maurice just liked to ring bells, church bells, hand bells, any bells really, as his father had done, catching buses all over Derbyshire to whichever church required him. Maurice had picked up the hobby and, as he tended to with hobbies, opted for full immersion.

Bell-ringing, though indoors and stationary, seemed related to sailing. Both involved ropes, technical language, and a gratifying combination of skill and knowledge. Precision was essential. The bells were rung in rounds or in a series of sequences known as rows and changes. Mastery was possible by extensive memorisation, which suited Maurice. He liked to tell people about the mathematical possibilities. On eight bells you can ring 40,320 different changes; on twelve, more than 479 million. He composed his own ringings, which he wrote out by hand and kept in a special folder.

The other ringers in the New Forest were something approaching friends. Colleagues, more like. A mixed assortment, mostly retired, and all people, like him, who gained satisfaction from an exacting, niche hobby. Maurice didn't talk much. They presumed he was shy. When he did attempt to socialise, he seemed to gravitate towards the women more than the men. Even so, if they all went for dinner together after a practice, he'd usually refuse to go along. If he was persuaded to join them, he'd struggle to hear the conversation, complain, and leave early.

FIVE

We talk about the dead to keep them alive. The conversation tends to work better with people who knew them too. To anyone else the dead are fictitious. A name, a picture, an anecdote about something they once did or said, but nothing close to flesh and warmth and movement. It's hard, in the middle of grief, to clearly describe the person you miss. Sometimes you can't even see them, or remember what they sounded like. If you look too hard at a memory, it dissolves.

Maurice wanted to talk about her all the time. She was the *only* thing he wanted to talk about, but when it came to it, when he was in company, he hardly spoke of her at all. It wasn't just the lack of people to talk to. Somehow, he couldn't ever express what he felt, or not in a way that seemed to make sense or would adequately represent her. He worried about boring people.

What was there to say? Trapped inside a person, grief can

feel like a rising tide of water, something vast and dramatic requiring release. But once spoken, it tends to reveal itself to be the same, small essential things, over and over. He missed her. He struggled without her. He wished she were still there.

~

It was obvious, really. He would write her into existence; he would build her out of words.

Maurice had kept writing, even when no one was paying him to write anymore. Their second book, *Second Chance: Voyage to Patagonia*, published in 1977, had come and gone without much interest. Greenfield, the literary agent, had been right. A long, granular account of a successful sailing voyage was not as exciting as a shipwreck.

There were no more books after that, apart from Maralyn's *Galley Handbook*, published in 1978. The small volume contained recipes for everything from boiled beetroot to apple sponge, and a chapter on "the complexities of provisioning." Its audience can't have been large.

Maurice kept writing, though. It's hard to stop, once you've acquired the habit. On the page, he could say things he didn't seem able to say out loud. It was calm there, and in his control. Once he told a friend, "I write essays, and because nobody reads my essays, I send them as letters to people."

He took the craft seriously, drafting and redrafting and consulting a dictionary to use the most elaborate words he could find. The end result was typed out in full and signed by hand in ink. *Yours ever, Maurice.* His letters were extremely long. Every year, on Maurice's birthday, June took him a small present and Maurice wrote to thank her. Pages and pages. Often, she'd still be wading through the previous one when the next one arrived.

He even wrote letters to Jamie, who lived next door and whom he saw most days. Maurice was so wedded to the ceremony of letter writing that instead of delivering the letter himself, he put a stamp on it and took it to the nearest postbox.

A year after Maralyn died, Maurice suggested an idea to B. He could write her a series of letters about Maralyn, telling the stories of their adventures at sea. B. might not want to live with him, but she could hardly object to being written to. That was the other good thing about letters: No one can stop you from writing them. No one can interrupt.

~

Maurice wrote his first letter to B. on 14 May 2003.

> *This is the letter I have been threatening to write to you for some little time.*

Threatening!

> *But why write a letter, I can hear you ask, when we have such regular congenial contact? Well, in a peculiar sort of way, I feel a need to gather some of my memories of Maralyn and set them down on paper before they become dim and distorted. . . .*
>
> *Inevitably, because of the poignancy of my memories, it is apt to become protracted, for which I apologise.*

He did warn her.

The words didn't come easily, as if they ever do, but still, he piled them on top of each other, as though if he used enough of them, they might add up to the truth. It was hard for a mind like Maurice's to accept the approximation of language.

Every story is a series of choices: what to include, what to leave out. Each selection or omission distorts the material. Maurice, disturbed by such imprecision, wanted to write their lives as if seen from above by some godly, all-seeing eye, uncorrupted by his own presence. He couldn't understand why it seemed so difficult to erase himself from the story of their life.

He was getting older; his memory was no longer reliable. Scenes and images rose and fell away like the tides. Somewhere among them was the truth, but it was impossible to say exactly where. Maralyn had always been his witness. Partners corroborate. Without her, he had no one to verify his account. What he was writing, therefore, was inherently untrustworthy. How strange that he ever thought it could be otherwise.

~

Twenty-five letters followed the first. Twenty-five long letters, written every few weeks from May 2003 to December 2004. Sometimes, on a good run, he'd write a few in quick succession, a fortnight in between. Then a pause, like in the summer of 2004, when he had a string of bad colds.

Thousands and thousands of words. Day after day in the little box room, tapping at the keys. It became his job. He was writing his third book, he realised. Each letter would be a chapter.

His first two books had been written rapidly, under pressure of deadlines and almost entirely without reflection. Now he could take his time. There was no publisher impatiently waiting for his manuscript. There was no hope of a publisher at all. He had a proposed readership of one, maybe two. Maurice was writing nominally for B., but really he was writing for himself.

Out came the charts, the diary, the logbooks. To narrate the course of their travels, he had to study them all again. He spent day after day lost in the events of thirty years ago, reading every word Maralyn had written. Writing about her wasn't so much a distraction from his grief as an immersion in it. He was with her all the time, re-creating every day of their voyages. It gave his grief occupation. The problem was when he reached the end of a chapter, looked up from the page, and realised she wasn't there.

20 August 2003: Before, there was always something to come but, for the present, only loneliness and sad thoughts move in. Have you known this too? I am not an explorer imagining that being alone is my discovery. Others before us have discovered that desolate landfall.

The metaphor made sense. Being alone was like returning to land. In an overpopulated town on the south coast of England, Maurice was lonelier than he had ever been on a life raft in the middle of an ocean with his wife.

~

Lives tend to start in one place and end somewhere else. One thing after another. Maurice wanted to avoid chronology, perhaps finding it too obvious. Or maybe it felt too brutal, because it can end only one way. A person's last phase is often cruel. Maralyn's was.

Maurice began at the beginning, or at least his chosen beginning, which was the moment Mike Morton asked him to take his place at a car rally. Life worthy of record began with Maralyn. And life worthy of record *with* Maralyn was their life on boats.

His childhood, parents, siblings, and schooling are barely mentioned, as if they never existed. The army is dealt with in a sentence. The "squandered decade" living alone in Derby is touched on only for its lack of meaning. Maurice chose the story he wanted to tell, the one that mattered to him, the story of their adventures at sea. All in all, about four years out of a forty-year marriage.

The years after the long voyages he passed through just as quickly. They sailed round the Mediterranean, put their boat up for charter, and worked on her as crew. Briefly, they lived in Spain and thought about moving there for good.

Towards the end of the penultimate letter, writing about the end of their time in Spain, Maurice recounts how Maralyn suddenly fell ill. They sailed to Gibraltar, where she saw a doctor and discovered, to their amazement, that she was pregnant. There were complications. Maralyn had to return to England on the next flight and be taken to hospital by June, while Maurice sailed the boat home.

"The outcome," wrote Maurice, "was that Maralyn's pregnancy was terminated, the foetus malformed and dead." That's it. A single line for the child they never had, or wanted. Later, when Maralyn was dying, she used to talk about this child to Pat. She would sit up in bed in the middle of the night and wonder who the child might have been, and whether they would have taken care of her now.

~

On the last page of his last letter, Maurice wrote of their decision to sell *Auralyn II.* They were back in Lymington; Maralyn was working at a garden centre, then for a company selling wood-burning stoves. Maurice was running a chandlery in Lymington called Yot Grot, selling odds and ends for boats. They were back on land, just like everyone else. A bungalow, a dog, a garden. The return to England had been permanent: There had been a large tax bill, and they couldn't afford to keep the boat. It fell to Maralyn to make the final, fateful decision on *Auralyn II*'s disposal.

Of course it did. Losing the boat, like last time, was the greatest loss. They'd always said their boats were their family, their children.

Once she was sold, *Auralyn II* left England within weeks. Three years later, they heard she had completed a voyage of sixty thousand miles and ended up in New Zealand, of all places.

SIX

Everything was ready. Maurice had exchanged multiple letters with his solicitor and gone over his will and the lasting power of attorney. He'd had his loft insulated and his gutters replaced. He'd checked and rechecked the strongboxes he kept in the attic and written an inventory of all the items they contained, including some large knives he'd been given in South Korea. He had decided, very precisely, who would get what. It was like the performance they used to go through before setting sail: packing and repacking, endless lists. Maurice prepared for death as if he were preparing for an ocean voyage.

Except death didn't seem to be in a particular hurry. The doctor found cancer in his prostate, but not severe enough to threaten his life. Maurice told Jamie, his neighbour, almost in disappointment, that the disease wasn't likely to kill him. He'd have to wait for something else.

Finally, he became unwell. Something was wrong with his kidney. His doctor referred him to Southampton General Hospital, where he declined quickly. He was moved to a hospice, the doctors thinking he had only days to live, and spent those days typing on his laptop. He didn't die. The hospice said they couldn't keep him, because he was taking up space for people who really did need to die, so they moved him again, to a nursing home.

The hospice had suited Maurice: The staff were kind, the atmosphere peaceful. It happened to be opposite Erroll Bruce's old house, where they'd stayed when they came back to England in 1973. The lane on which it stood led down to the marshes and lagoons, home of geese and lapwings and curlews, and then to the sea. At the lane's end, the sky opens out and the light changes, thinned and brightened by the water.

In the home, back in the confines of town, he was surrounded by dementia patients. Maurice was physically ailing but mentally sound. He preferred to stay in his room. Upstairs, a communal area was decorated like a Caribbean beach, with a blue sky and tropical sea. He refused to go in. It must have seemed ridiculous, and painful, when you'd known the real thing.

While he was in the home, Jamie came to visit and took him out in a wheelchair on excursions round Lymington. Maurice found it awkward being out in public in his chair. All those genteel people, pottering over the cobbles to the little shops. He worried, too, about falling out if Jamie hit a kerb.

In the autumn, before it got too cold, Jamie took him farther, to the cliffs along the coast. A paved path runs along the top, and Jamie pushed Maurice along in his chair, bundled up in a blanket to keep him warm in the sea breeze. From the path, they could look down at the shingle beach, across the grey water of the Solent to the Needles, a row of long, thin rocks that stick out of the sea next to the Isle of Wight.

Maurice had sailed this stretch with Maralyn so many times. He was more used to admiring the view from the water, at speed, passing the stillness of the land while he travelled somewhere else. Now he was the still point, looking out.

~

Slowly, slowly, his body gave way. He slept more, until he was sleeping nearly all the time.

In mid-December, Jean and Dave, his friends from the Lyndhurst teahouse, came to see him. They hadn't known him well, but they'd grown fond of him over time, noticed he'd stopped coming to the teahouse, and wondered how he was. Maurice told them he was ready to go. He seemed utterly relieved.

The next day, 15 December 2017, he died. It had all taken a little longer than he'd hoped.

~

The instructions left for Colin and June were very clear. No ceremony, for a start. His ashes should be scattered at the Naked Man. They arranged a date, and told a few people he'd known—Jamie, his cleaner, the bell ringers—but realised that they didn't know many of these people by sight. June turned up at the car park in the New Forest holding a handmade sign printed with Maurice's name.

Once the small group had gathered, they walked along the path together to the tree. June said a few words. Then they scattered him, his ashes falling on the earth that had absorbed his wife and his dog.

Sorting out his things, they found the drawer of cream napkins from the tearoom. It wasn't clear why he'd kept them. Maurice had requested that the bungalow be emptied and its contents properly disposed of, not left out on the street to be taken. He asked for his hard drives to be destroyed, too, as if he wanted to leave no trace.

In the study, they found cardboard boxes full of copies of his final book, a self-published collection of the letters he wrote to B. Colin and June wondered if the local museum in Lymington might like them, being a record of a local life both remarkable and unremarkable, like any life, but surely containing something more notable than usual. A story worth preserving.

The museum didn't want them. In the end, they took the books to a charity shop where the assistant said it might be better to share them with a few other shops in the area because it was unlikely they'd be able to shift multiple copies of the same book.

~

There are many ways to take the measure of a life. In the linear version, Maurice's life had a hard beginning, a dramatic middle, an isolated end. An end somehow encapsulated by the image of piles of his unread memoir stacked in the musty back rooms of charity shops along the south coast of England. But this doesn't seem quite fair. After all, he wrote that book to remember Maralyn. It was work for its own sake. Not everything has to be seen.

In any case, they're not always right, these lines we draw to make sense of our lives, or the lives of others.

In November 2003, Maurice was in the middle of one of his long colds. For three weeks he'd been unable to sit at his computer, incapable of concentrating or writing anything that made sense. The late autumn was closing in, the days reducing. His vision seemed to narrow in tandem. Within weeks, he'd be lost in those spirals of self-defeating thought, writing of his failure to help Maralyn at the end of her life, his failure to do her justice after her death, the failures looping round each other until he was tied and bound. Before his mind turned on itself, he realised something:

> *Although I am wary of accepted truths, I believe in all human beings there is a desire to love and be loved, to experience the full fierceness of human emotion, and to make it a measure of the success of one's life. For me to write about Maralyn's life is the most reliable way I can keep faith with this receding notion.*

It was rare for him, this kind of clarity. But here was a way to evaluate existence. Measure its success by the extent to which you have loved and been loved.

On that count, his life had been a triumph.

Epilogue

MAURICE: Do you get paid for this?

ALVARO: No, I don't get paid for this, it's for people with a passion for castaways. They like to watch castaways.

MAURICE: I see. Oh dear, oh dear, oh dear. And what do you do if you find the camera isn't working halfway through, do you have to start it all over again?

~

Shortly before he died, Maurice gave an interview to a young Spanish filmmaker called Alvaro Cerezo, a collector of castaway stories and explorer of desert islands. Alvaro had come all the way from Spain to talk to Maurice, much to Maurice's amazement. They met in a busy pub, noisy with the chat of drinkers.

Maurice found it almost impossible to hear what Alvaro was saying.

> ALVARO: I want to ask about fishing.
>
> MAURICE: Fitness?
>
> ALVARO: [*louder*] Fishing. When the raft was drifting first, fishing was not possible. Why?
>
> MAURICE: No. I'm so sorry, I wish I could hear better than this.

Maralyn would have given a better interview, Maurice told Alvaro. In fact, once he'd turned up his hearing aid, Maurice did just fine. He covered everything: the whale, fishing, turtles, boobies, sharks, flares, rescue. He recalled specific, vivid moments, such as how Maralyn liked to put her finger on the noses of the sharks as they swam past.

Some of the stories he'd told endlessly, in television interviews, newspaper articles, three books, countless talks at yacht clubs. But stories get forgotten.

> ALVARO: You disappeared from the media. You changed your life and we didn't see your face anymore.
>
> MAURICE: Well, that's quite true. When Maralyn died, I just left it all.

Maurice told Alvaro things he'd never mentioned in any of his books. Small things, like how they'd become obsessed with drinking milkshakes when they got to Hawaii, and big things, like the awfulness of his childhood.

MAURICE: Until I met Maralyn, I didn't know what affection was.

ALVARO: You were really in love with Maralyn.

MAURICE: Well, if that's what you call it, yes. It might sound a bit soppy, but yes.

At one point, Alvaro asked Maurice if he wished it had never happened: the sinking, the life raft, the whole fandango.

Maurice considered the question. Yes, part of him would want to spare himself such an ordeal. But if he could do it all again in the knowledge that someone would rescue him after four months, then he would. It was the farthest he had ever been from civilisation, which was all he'd ever wanted. And how else would he have had the experience of living in the ocean, among the fish and the birds, so close to a whale that he could look into the darkness of its enormous eye?

After a while, Alvaro seemed to sense something in Maurice, an absence that surrounded him, like an aura.

ALVARO: So you have no family, nothing.

MAURICE: I'm quite happy.

ALVARO: Do you feel lonely?

MAURICE: Oh yes, it's a lonely life, but I'm happy being lonely, I think.

There was no point in dwelling on his loneliness. It had been with him all along. The form it took now was only a logical consequence of the loss of the person he loved.

Without pause, apropos of nothing, Maurice returned to the sight of the whale:

> *I don't know whether you can really imagine what it's like to be sitting on a life raft and a whale comes up close to you. It's such a treat to see this docile whale alongside you, and it did nothing, it just stared at us. This whale sat there, and it sat there for a long time, twenty minutes, half an hour. I got to know it very well, and then it suddenly went off very slowly, glided away, and then it dived, not a splash. It was marvellous, just to see that.*

It was marvellous, just to see that.

When he remembers the whale, something happens to Maurice's face, as if memory were at work on it, love too, reanimating. His eyes brighten with tears. He is with her again, next to her, time dissolved. After so long untold, the encounter is real, vivid, as if happening in the moment of telling, an earlier self and a present self somehow folding together so that all experience is current and the dead are alive.

Author's Note

I came across the story of Maurice and Maralyn while researching an article about people who choose to live on water. It was during the pandemic, mid-lockdown, and I'd become interested in people who decided to abandon conventional, land-based life and live on barges or cruise ships or experimental pods in the Pacific Ocean. I wasn't particularly looking for a shipwreck story or a sailing story—I have never been sailing—but the Baileys' experience struck me, not only in its extremity, but in the particular ways they survived. They wanted to escape, alone and unburdened, free to do what they liked. And yet it was only through a reliance on each other and the intervention of others—through interdependence—that they lived. The account in this book is based on multiple sources, chiefly the Baileys' own books: *117 Days Adrift*; *Second Chance: Voyage to Patagonia*; *The Galley Handbook*; and *When the Water Becomes Still*. Also, Maralyn's diary of 1973, kept by Maurice and shown to Alvaro Cerezo, who photographed every page (it is available to read on Alvaro's website, paradise.docastaway.com).

Other sources include the filmed interview between Alvaro and Maurice (an excerpt is available to view on the Docastaway YouTube channel); and my own interviews, in person or over email, with Colin Foskett, Terry Smith, Alvaro Cerezo, Bob Bailey, Pat Brewin, Ivor Davis, Sheila Skitt, Denis and Marion Baylis, Polly Osborne, Nita Dellamura, Hilary Brand, Jean and Dave Croucher, and Jamie Pope.

Material was also gathered from the extensive media coverage of their rescue and international tours found in the newspaper archives of the British Library, the British Newspaper Archive, international broadcast archive research conducted by Gregor Murbach, recordings, photos, and DVDs of interviews kept by Maurice and given to Colin Foskett, and an archive of Korean media coverage, including Captain Suh's thirteen-part account in *The Korea Times*, collated by Matt VanVolkenburg on his blog, *Gusts of Popular Feeling.*

Thank you to all these people and institutions for their generosity and help, particularly Colin Foskett, who drove me round the New Forest to visit Maurice and Maralyn's various homes and who walked with me to the Naked Man, where their ashes were scattered.

Acknowledgments

Thank you to my agent, Chris Wellbelove, early believer, close reader, anxiety wrangler; and to my American editor, Jynne Dilling, who read with the most generous eye and was up for the adventure.

At Riverhead, further thanks to Geoff Kloske, Ashley Garland, Nora Alice Demick, Helen Yentus, Bianca Flores, and Afarin Allabakhshizadeh.

And thank you to Gideon Lewis-Kraus for his instinctive generosity and for sending a text.

At Chatto & Windus and Vintage: thank you to my editor, Becky Hardie, who steered the boat so coolly through the tunnel, Asia Choudhry for her layers of skill, Rowena Skelton-Wallace, Susanne Hillen, Eugenie Woodhouse, Yeti Lambregts, Jessica Spivey, Katrina Northern, and Bryan Angus. And at Aitken Alexander: Emily Fish, Lisa Baker, Anna Hall, Alex Bil-Watrobska, Vickie Dillon, and Laura Otal. For love, friendship, reading, encouragement, sanity, conversation, sailing knowledge, in some cases employment, and in other cases helping to raise my kids, thank you to Celia Elmhirst, Rechenda Fleming, Tom Elmhirst, Claudia Baughan and their families; Joanna Lamont, Matt Lamont, Susanna Hislop, Katie Waldegrave, Chris Clothier, Jot Davies, Laura Hamm, Isabel Powles, Rosie Tomkins, Felix Leworthy, Tara Wondraczek, Sam Hodges, Sophie Vickers, Tara Alhadeff, Iradj Bagherzade, Clemency Burton-Hill, Tom Basden, Megan Walsh, Claudia Renton, Sarah Jacobs, Flo Phillips, Mark Richards, Hannah Westland, Stuart McGurk, Nat Luurtsema, David Wolf, Sam Knight, Jonathan Beckman, Penny Martin, Helena Lee, Lily Harper, Opal Harper, Brookfield Primary School, and the Childcare Emergencies WhatsApp group.

Thank you, and with all my love, always, to Cleo Lamont and Daniel Lamont.

And to Tom Lamont. Lucky to be adrift with you.